Sushi in Cortez
Interdisciplinary Essays on Mesa Verde

Edited by David Taylor and Steve Wolverton
Foreword by Catherine S. Fowler

The University of Utah Press
Salt Lake City

The University of Utah Press gratefully acknowledges the financial support of the following, which helped make this publication possible:

The Association for the Study of Literature and Environment

University of Minnesota–Duluth Chancellor's Small Grant.

 The Defiance House Man colophon is a registered trademark of the University of Utah Press. It is based on a four-foot-tall Ancient Puebloan pictograph (late PIII) near Glen Canyon, Utah.

19 18 17 16 15   1 2 3 4 5

CIP Data on File with the Library of Congress.

   ISBN 978-1-60781-412-2 (paper)
   ISBN 978-1-60781-413-9 (e-book)

All photographs by Steve Bardolph unless otherwise specified.

Printed and bound by Sheridan Books, Inc., Ann Arbor, Michigan.

Sushi in Cortez

Contents

Foreword

English, like all living languages, has the internal mechanisms for speakers to produce new forms or words to embody new thoughts and ideas. In this case, although the term *interdisciplinarity* does not roll off my tongue easily (a decision by an academic committee, perhaps?), the underlying concept it expresses lies at the heart of this volume. In it six people from six different backgrounds and disciplines describe in six stunning and thought-provoking essays and various visual media a common journey to a place—Mesa Verde and vicinity in southwestern Colorado. The experience proved to be both highly inter- (or trans-) disciplinary and at the same time transformative for each—as I feel it will be for their readers.

"Interdisciplinary programs" and "interdisciplinary studies" have been around for quite some time in academic settings. Most have involved either team-teaching by people from different disciplines, individuals teaching subject matter that is the shared purview of several departments but rarely taught, or both. They tend to attract faculty and students who do not like to have their interests pigeonholed into one or two disciplines or who want genuine cross-disciplinary experiences. Some courses are taught only once—or a few times—as experiments. Others, along with programs, have more staying power. But many have disappeared for a variety of reasons, some because "once or twice" was enough, a few because they became part of a regular curriculum somewhere. Others were victims of ever-shrinking budgets for "experiments," some for lack of a true interdisciplinary focus or ethic, and certainly some over squabbles as to who gets or how to count the "FTEs" (academic-speak for which faculty member and what department get credit for the teaching and enrollment—an issue of ROI [see Steve W., this volume]). Perhaps yet others have also failed for lack of a truly focused interdisciplinary or transdisci-plinary experience for the faculty or students or both.

This experiment attempted to remedy the latter situation. Each of the participants (some already friends or at least acquaintances) was ready for something different. Each showed a willingness to share his or her disci-plinary perspectives but at the same time suspend his or her beliefs that theirs was the only way of seeing. Each was ready not only to listen and learn from the others, but also to dig deeper into self and be changed by the experience. The experiment proved highly successful, not only for the six people who chronicle their involvements here, but also because of the impacts on their subsequent work. At least one person (Steve B.) provides data on a follow-up project in his own local setting. I suspect that there will be more.

How much of the success of this particular project might have been due to the selection of these particular participants? We cannot know for sure, though I suspect quite a bit, which is not to say that similar teams involving other players with other interests could not be assembled suc-cessfully and involve themselves in other places or subjects. Although of varying ages, all are energetic, capable, and well entrenched and respected in their fields. It was therefore assumed by all that each would have some-thing very valuable to contribute. The team-building process did not hap-pen overnight: each had to decide on his or her role, as well as explore each other's personalities, ways of seeing, and knowledge. Each had to be willing and able to engage the place chosen: Mesa Verde and vicin-ity. Most had at least been there; some had fairly extensive experience; for one, there were deep ancestral ties. The latter person (Porter S.) and his perspective proved to be invaluable to all, and it is clear that the experi-ence would not have been nearly as successful without him.

How much of the success of the project had to do with the selection of place, Mesa Verde and vicinity, especially given Mesa Verde's Ancestral Puebloan heritage? Again, I suspect, quite a bit—although I can see this type of experience happening for other groups in other settings. For me, as an anthropologist and ethnobiologist, I can see it happening in a num-ber of other places in the indigenous world, certainly other World Heri-tage locations, and in a variety of environmental settings. But, like Steve W., I have also been moved by Mesa Verde and the Four Corners coun-try since an early age (fifteen). I have returned many times—in fact every chance I get—and have always found it special, in recent years in spite of heavy tourism, increased noise, and environmental degradation (especially unmanaged forests). My favorite times there are when I am alone, or with an indigenous person, who always reminds me that place is more significant than time. To respect a place, one must stop, look, and listen. Places, even old ones, are still living, and none are "abandoned." For me, respect and knowledge go hand in hand (see various authors herein), and I am not sure that I would place one before the other. Both are essential, and they grow together.

It is often said by ethnologists that fieldwork with and among other people changes you far more than it affects them. At the same time, a fieldworker also hopes to do no harm—but how can one ever be sure? Our late colleague Warren d'Azevedo always said that good living and learning were about "others knowing others." To this I would add, they are also about "others knowing places." If it takes interdisciplinarity to do that, I'm all for it.

Catherine S. Fowler
Foundation Professor Emerita
University of Nevada, Reno

Rock stairs along a path at Mesa Verde National Park.

Prologue

It's simple, what we have done in this book. We have engaged in what some might describe as "an organic process of spontaneous creativity." We were to "go to the field together" in order to experience something (anything) through the varied lenses of our disciplines and cultures, to share it, and to see how it affects each of us. It became an experiment in interdisciplinarity. We conducted this experiment in the Mesa Verde region of southwestern Colorado, where we visited Ancient Pueblo archaeological sites together. Archaeology in rough form has been the subject matter, the idea being that creative scholars would see the cultural landscape of Mesa Verde in diverse ways through the various lenses of their training and culture.

It's just not that simple, and what makes the process of creating this book complicated is the contemporary social context of the American university. A field experiment in interdisciplinarity (focused on archaeology or not) is difficult to explain in contemporary academia. Returning from the field to our everyday lives has been complicated because people ask questions: Where did you go? Who was on the team? Why was he or she on the team and not him or her? Why did the team choose to go to archaeological sites in the Mesa Verde region? What roles did team members play? How did the research develop? What was the "research" about? And, most important, what will the products of the project be? To be frank, the questions about this project from our colleagues and friends center on "Why would you do that?"

To answer that question, we offer this book. The prologue discusses some broad concerns about the challenges of interdisciplinarity, brief biographies, and an explanation about our choice of archaeology in the

Mesa Verde region as our subject. Also, we provide a chronology of our interviews, trips, and products to clarify our group's complicated history. The authors answer other questions in their individual chapters, such as what products they envision and why they joined the team and, importantly, how this project has shaped them.

WHY SUSHI? WHY CORTEZ?

Sushi in Cortez is an unconventional book born of an odd idea; researched in Skype conferences, freezing rain, brewpubs, long drives, and Ancient Pueblo sites; and written from perspectives that may or may not blend as easily as a reader may hope. It is not an academic work or a scholarly treatise on interdisciplinarity. Our group believes that those scholars who have long toiled within their fields and may have felt the claustrophobia of their disciplines and the narrow kinds of products they are allowed to list at the top of their curriculum vitaes will recognize a lost love of research and writing—curiosity, humility, and meeting others with passion and intelligence, no matter their disciplines or cultural backgrounds.

The book is irreverent because we did not research "how to do it." We did not read up on how to be interdisciplinary. It has been a purely inductive exercise, a plunge into cross-cultural and cross-disciplinary communication. It has been at times baffling, trying, and meandering. We have hit "Enter" on more e-mails asking for details and explanations than one can imagine. However, some of those same interchanges have also been intellectually beautiful. Those moments reminded us of the time, most likely when we were students, when our research was infused with our person.

We are unapologetic because we know that something is amiss in the academy and that places for the wildly curious are few. What is it we hope to offer our students? A command of the specialization of our fields? That's a given. What do we want to emulate? A huge, fiery, engaged passion for knowledge, work, and creativity, embracing all its possibilities. We hope this book shows something of that.

WHO ARE WE?

Steve Wolverton's scholarship is an amalgamation of ecology, anthropology, and archaeology. Although he finds the human past fascinating, Steve W. is also concerned about conservation of the "great outdoors," a term he uses because people constantly remind him that pristine wilderness does not exist during the Anthropocene. Further, in his view humans are not segregated from the environment; culture and nature are interwoven, for better or worse. His main concern is how do we interweave better? Steve W. loves science; he sees it as a powerful tool for knowing more things about the world, but he acknowledges its limits. His role in this project is to facilitate opportunities for encountering Mesa Verde by the members of the team.

David Taylor is a writer; he'll write about anything, including human nature, natural humans, or unnatural culture, via prose or poetry. He dives into topics ranging from natural science to music, often challenging genre forms, such as creative nonfiction, essay, and poetry. David wants to engage people through poetry and prose and hopes it makes a difference in the world concerning the global and local environmental crises. On this project, David is "the humanist" who explores archaeological sites in the Mesa Verde region through poetry. He and Steve Wolverton initiated the *Sushi in Cortez* project.

Steve Bardolph is an artist whose medium is nature and wilderness photography (even if it's not pristine). Others have made him into a graphic designer so that they can employ him to be a university professor. However, his mind belongs in three places: the field, photographing; the studio, creating wild panoramic vistas; and the classroom, stripping students of convention. He entered the Mesa Verde Project to encounter archaeological phenomena (landscapes and sites) through the lens of photographic arts. He understands the role that a design perspective can play in making an unwieldy assemblage of creative products mesh into a whole. His role on this team is to provide panoramic perspective.

Melinda Levin is a documentary filmmaker who delves into human-environmental relationships focusing on issues from how to ranch sustainably to why humankind should care for rivers. Embedded in her work is a series of tensions between the creative and perceptions of truth, which she'll admit is relative. She'll ask, can a story be told that is creative, honest, and truthful at the same time? Working with this group provides no road map, and her role here is to plop into the context of site visits in the Mesa Verde region and to simply create; she represents one of the creative artists on the team. However, she also brings a wealth of experience in terms of communicating science and communicating with scientists to the table, in addition to a propensity to leap cultural contexts and come back inspired to create stories through film. David Taylor and Steve Wolverton invited her to the team early in its history.

Porter Swentzell is a person of two worlds; he straddles Pueblo and mainstream American cultures, effectively engaging both, risking belonging to neither. He is deeply concerned with the future of the traditions (culturally private and public ones) of Pueblo peoples. But he recognizes that the worlds he straddles need each other, so he offers a helping hand to both. Porter teaches most of the time, whether it be in the university classroom, the living room, or during a Mesa Verde hike. Porter's role in this project is to tell a Pueblo story about Mesa Verde archaeology to the other team members. In so doing, he has inadvertently and respectfully played the role of antagonist. Through our shared yet conflicted history and via our cultural similarities and differences, he has held up a mirror that each of us has looked into at times with horror, but also with appreciation.

Robert Figueroa is an environmental philosopher, which means that he is concerned with the stories we tell ourselves about humans meshed with landscapes, environments, and multiple cultures. His work focuses on how to encounter environmental injustice through frameworks in which members of disparate cultures gaze upon conflicting issues and upon each other and gain awareness. Through this process, perhaps the propensity for consideration and cooperation can grow. His role on this team is to be a contrarian; like Porter, he serves as a mirror, but more assertively, as he has been charged with the antistories, things that we miss through being comfortable within our own disciplines, perceiving through our own lenses.

The *Sushi in Cortez* team formed through a series of conversations. In the chapters the team members share how they developed the role they played; however, each also conveys to the reader how the experience shaped scholarship in their disciplines.

How Sushi in Cortez Began

The story of how we settled on visiting archaeological sites is humorous, sad, possibly courageous, or maybe foolish, depending on your perspective. More than four years ago, a few of us began to talk about how we might work together. Our initial conversations were based on relationships and friendships—on collaboration first and subject matter second. As we tried to convey something about our fields, we came back again and again to the premise that we are all storytellers. We were intrigued by questions such as "What makes a poem legitimate to a poet, an argument compelling to a philosopher, a film convincing and engaging . . . ?" and so forth across our careers and disciplines. This led to our first presentation, an interdisciplinary panel on research as storytelling at the 2010 annual Society of Ethnobiology Conference in Victoria, BC. Whatever comfort we had gained in giving this collective panel was quickly lost; we were shaken out of it by a direct question by a frustrated listener who wondered out loud if we were not just doing warmed-over academics while touting that we were doing more. There, we became students again.

A vivid recollection for the four members of the Mesa Verde team who served on that panel (Robert Figueroa, Melinda Levin, David Taylor, and Steve Wolverton) was that we were in the midst of having great fun discussing storytelling with members of the audience; a First Nations man raised his hand and conveyed that he was offended by what we were doing. To paraphrase, he stated that he "had come to this panel because his people have real-world problems and are trying to face current environmental crises; he had hoped to gain tools from our panel to help him, and he felt he had gained nothing but anecdotes and intimation that he was clearly outside the academy, offered mainly from Texans." Each of us reacted differently to this criticism. Melinda and Rob, the filmmaker and environmental philosopher, respectively, were thankful. Steve W. was at first threatened, David Taylor was surprised, and perhaps we all felt a bit misunderstood. The question, though, was rightly sobering. Are we just doing old academics while saying we're doing something new?

We let that experience marinate for nearly eight months. During our break, we would see each other, but there was no real impetus to move forward as a team during 2010. That changed when Julie West, a media professional at the University of North Texas (UNT), wanted to interview us about the panel and to publish a podcast about our experiences together.

By the time of the podcast interviews (there were two interview sessions with Julie West), each of us had reflected upon our Victoria panel. What we found is that we had indeed been humbled and in fact felt even more dedicated to exploration of research in stuffy paradigms as simple storytelling. Then came the critical question from Julie West to shepherd us forward: "What do you plan to do next?"

Good question. Our immediate reaction to Julie's question was that we should go to the field together and see what happens when different storytellers with different media approach the same place. What makes our project different from many other interdisciplinary projects is that we did not form a team to solve a problem. We did the opposite: we created a team that had become highly interactive and trusting, and we therefore wanted to work together. This harkened back to something primal for each of us, the native explorer in our humanity, like Darwin, Thoreau, Carson, even E. O. Wilson, scholars from a different time.

Why Mesa Verde?

Proximity to the Mesa Verde region made it an easy choice for those of us from UNT. Steve W. had interned and worked at Crow Canyon Archaeological Center in Cortez, Colorado, for some years. Melinda owns a home not far away, and Rob and David had taught and worked on research projects in the area not long before. Steve W. came to know of Porter through Crow Canyon and invited Steve B. to join us to add a photographer's perspective.

Mesa Verde had several ingredients for a perfect collaboration: breathtaking landscapes, intriguing archaeological questions about past cultures, beautiful archaeological sites, contemporary cooperation with Native Puebloans, historical and contemporary conflict between archaeologists, American society in general, and national and international tourism. Elements include cultural discord, consumerism, hard science and frequently soft reason, water availability and use, public and private land disputes, institutions, agencies, and management folk. These are the stuff of science, white papers, federal grants, the National Environmental Policy Act (NEPA), and other forms of policy and creative expression. We did not know what stories we would tell upon venturing into the Mesa Verde region, but we knew that there were stories to tell.

The choice of looking into the Mesa Verde region also allowed us to ask deeper questions about history and culture, not only about Ancient Puebloans but also about the industry built around engaging their former homes and communities. Just as important, we had to ask ourselves wonderful and painful questions about our own engagement, our distance, our concepts of cultural respect, our tourism, and our desires for an authentic experience. For example, entering an Ancient Pueblo site such as Sand Canyon, Yucca House, or Goodman Point is a demanding experience for the nonexpert. Oh, interpretive signs by the Park Service offer images, maps, and archaeological evidence about the piles of rubble and rock, but there is no ranger nearby to offer stories, sweep her hand from one horizon to the next filling in the gaps with stories about water, warfare, religion, or family. Signs ask the visitor to respect the site and not shift the rocks, not to pick up the remnant potsherds, or to litter, but the Park Service trusts that you follow suit. If you stayed the entire day at any of the above sites, you'd see no more than five to ten people. Architecture at these sites has not been reconstructed to aid the eye and the mind. You're alone there—engaged deeply or totally lost; it's up to the visitor.

Head to Mesa Verde National Park (MVNP) or Hovenweep, and it's a totally different experience. Guided tours, buses of seniors and foreign tourists, cameras clicking at a dizzying speed, reconstructed dwellings, and signs saying where a visitor may or may not step, touch, or linger. You can descend into the darkness of a kiva with twenty or so others and get a description of its ancient secular and sacred use. But if in some ineffable way a visitor happens to have a moment of connection in this kiva, with these people, listening to that ranger, one has to ask, what is it that is happening? The past, the now, the desire for something authentic, something authentic despite the wrappings of tourism that keep one from authenticity, cultural distance, cultural empathy, and on and on? To lay claim to an experience of connection here is to briskly walk through a house of mirrors without ever bumping your head; you are (hopefully) aware of the thousands of false images and able to navigate them with wisdom. Or perhaps you close your eyes, walk forward, and get lucky. Most commonly, encountering these sites and the industry built around them brings the past to us and simultaneously distances us from it—"two ships passing in the night."

Mesa Verde National Park and many other Ancient Pueblo sites in the Four Corners region of the American Southwest provide engagement with the deep past for millions of "average Americans" each year. We suspect their senses of intrigue match our own; at parks such as Mesa Verde National Park and Chaco Canyon, the huge reconstructed dwellings and rich artifact records seem to make the past highly visible. However, in terms of archaeology, this lucidity is somewhat of a mirage. The archaeological record in the Southwest has a deep temporal and wide spatial expanse, covering extensive cultural change and diversity. Mobile hunter-gatherers occupied the region greater than ten thousand years ago and gradually came to finely tune their cultures to a rich harvest of arid environments. By roughly four thousand years ago, these hunter-gatherer societies began to coalesce into seasonally occupied villages. This may seem like a revolutionary shift, but cultural change in this case is more of a continuum, as people hunted and gathered seasonally while gradually adopting farming of corn, beans, and squash. Throw into this mix the eventual domestication of the turkey and the advent and subsequent evolution of various forms of pottery and architecture, not to mention the difficult-to-study but ever-mysterious civic and ceremonial practices of the people who lived in these villages. The stage is set for a fascinating archaeological story in the Mesa Verde region, which is even more compelling because at about AD 1300 people abruptly left the region. For Mesa Verde archaeology, the age-old question "Why did people do that?" applies to so many tangible contexts, which fascinates archaeologists, the American public, and folks from around the world.

With a past so clearly fascinating and enriching, an increasing number of archaeologists, Native persons, and tourists are either asking or being asked to engage the question "Whose past is it?" For some, this imbues Mesa Verde with a history of conquest, and depending on one's perspective this might have opposing meanings. For others, the past is shared, a story that no single person or culture can own. Certainly, our group of diverse scholars has not been able to avoid the question of heritage. Each of us encountered, approached, and engaged consideration of who owns the past differently. Truly, the archaeologist must give something away that he or she has claimed as his or her own to share the past with others. Perhaps the Native person must reclaim something others have taken, and tourists face the opportunity to understand the deeply multifaceted cultural heritage that Mesa Verde is to contemporary Pueblo people, well beyond the archaeologists' metric assessments of farming, building, and tool making in the past.

The irony of pondering questions of heritage is that humans face a challenging future together, whether or not we settle disputes from the past. The American West provides a canvas on which to build something new because the frontier has passed, leaving us together in its wake. However, academia has become so specialized that each of us is hard-pressed to do more than scribble separate renderings in uncommon languages next to one another. It is uncomfortable and perhaps embarrassing to realize that expertise in our small academic communities does not provide for a shared future and manifests mainly from a divided and conquered past. That is, we have each conquered our fields of study to varying degrees and in unique ways. How can we share the future from such disparate roots? From our comfort zones in which we see ourselves as experts, must we become novices in inter-disciplinarity and cross-cultural research? How humbling it is to begin anew, how necessary. Someone has to do it. That's what the stories in this book are about.

An Invitation

Readers of this collection of essays might feel as though they are reliv-ing the events of our group over and over through each of our points of view in Rashomon style. Our individual essays do cover some of the same events, but readers will see dramatically different perspectives on those events, our group, and what each gained from the experience. The editors requested each team member focus on his or her fears, frustrations, joys, epiphanies, losses, gains, and musings. Thus, a reader may wonder why he should read six reflections on the same "plot." The editors would answer that this is how such a group must first learn to work together; a common plotline offers a thread of common experience.

Perhaps an analogy would best describe this book. We were hungry for something outside the Hamburger Helper, rushed-evening fare of estab-lished paradigms, so we took a risk. We prepared a cross-cultural, interdis-ciplinary meal for ourselves because we were famished for enrichment. We asked each other to make a dish from his or her past, and we prepared them in the same kitchen at the same time. Then, as we cooked, a conversation happened as we shared utensils, borrowed herbs here and spices there, and asked how each other's dish was made. Then we sat down and ate together. We shared food, passed the bottle, told and listened to stories, and, impor-tantly, laughed. Now, we are telling you about how fun it was to be in the kitchen together, how wonderful the talk, and what a great dinner it was. This book asks you to sample this meal, not so that you can re-create it, but to entice you to make one of your own—with a group of your own making. The only advice we will offer is to make sure it is diverse, make sure each chef has humility, humor, and heart, and to be ready for flavors and combi-nations you may never have dreamed of. Bon appétit!

Chronology of Our Group's Work

May 2010—Steve, David, Melinda, and Rob present at the Society of Ethnobiology Conference, Victoria, BC

Spring 2011—Podcast interview with Julie West, "Science, Life, and Poli-tics: Tools for Legitimizing Stories"

July 23–27, 2011—First trip to Mesa Verde area: Steve W., Steve B., Porter, and David

October 5–10, 2011—Second trip to Mesa Verde area: Steve W., Steve B., Melinda, Rob, Porter, and David

March 29–30, 2012—"Mesa Verde Stories: Arts & Archaeology—a Presentation and Exhibition," UNT

April 13, 2012—"Sharing Mesa Verde Stories: Transdisciplinary Collaboration in the Field," Society of Ethnobiology Conference, Denver

Supplemental Material

A digital version of Steve Bardolph's two panoramic photos and Melinda Levin's full-length film can be found on the *Sushi in Cortez* book page at the University of Utah Press website, www.UofUpress.com.

Notes, additional photos, and other supplementary materials that relate to *Sushi in Cortez* are archived as supplementary material at OpenContext.org: Wolverton, Steve, David Taylor, Steve Bardolph, Robert Figueroa, Melinda Levin, Porter Swentzell. 2015. Essays from the Edge of Academia: Supplements to 'Sushi in Cortez'. Open Context. Audiovisual. <http://opencontext.org/projects/03828ABD-2B37-4B91-A592-4266B3DB2383> http://dx.doi.org/10.6078/M7FQ9TJ5"

1

Making Sushi and Producing the Mesa Verde Project

Steve Wolverton

I want to tell the story of how the process of engaging Mesa Verde archaeology unfolded within our interdisciplinary group; however, I need to start by describing the role that I played. The choice to go to the field together was going to *my* field together. Our team decided to take an introspective look at archaeology, not poetry, film, graphic design, or philosophy. There is considerable debate among archaeologists concerning what caused Mesa Verde abandonment at roughly AD 1300, and archaeologists have detailed stories to tell based on expertise, data, analysis, and discussion. My role in this project has been to suspend my own storytelling except for portraying the most basic framework of cultural history in the region. Did environmental change lead to abandonment, overpopulation, politics? I answered that archaeologists have defended each of these positions, but I refrained from sharing mine.

The point of diving into fieldwork together for most members of the team has been to see how the creative process is fueled when one is exposed to a variety of perspectives through a variety of lenses at the same time in the same contexts. We needed a playing field; archaeology represents an interesting and accessible venue. I must acknowledge in hindsight, however, the extreme difficulty I experienced at suspending my judgments about what happened during Mesa Verde's abandonment. In truth, this left me quite vulnerable because I opened myself up to the questions of how a filmmaker, a poet, or a photographer/designer frames the story of Mesa Verde archaeology when I do not provide detailed claims. More scary, how does a Pueblo person frame the story of what happened in prehistory?

I was suspending a process that I believe to be science, which has provided me with a power base in conversations about prehistory under the

Steve Wolverton and Porter Swentzell walk the trail at Hovenweep.

logic that "I know what happened because I have studied it diligently." I am an expert, and in many conversations I am *the* expert. In this group, I could have claimed that mantle, but the project is not about what archaeologists think. It is about what happens when scholars from different disciplines inductively immerse themselves into a new research context together. Many archaeologists would view this as a pointless exercise in frustration (at times I was frustrated along these lines). But through restraint, I found that a filmmaker, a poet, a Pueblo scholar, or a photographer does not focus on the same data and may not ask many of the same questions that I do, thereby bringing to light ideas previously unimaginable. I found that my colleagues see the story told by a Pueblo scholar to be equally believable and perhaps more interesting than the scientific information I provide about the past. I found that the Pueblo scholar has legitimate reasons underlying his claims about what happened in the past.

I listened, and it was difficult because they told their stories, not mine. If we had decided to make a film together or to collaboratively write poetry, then I would have experienced something much closer to what my colleagues did, which would be to enter a different field and bring my creative side to it. I imagine this would be disastrous, as what could an archaeologist bring to the art of poetry? I am certain that they felt similar frustrations as they entered archaeology, perhaps questioning what business they had being there. However, much fieldwork in archaeology is publicly funded, and Mesa Verde National Park, Chaco Canyon, and similar places in the Southwest are supported by and designed for public consumption. This team of interdisciplinary nonexperts represents a creative and intelligent segment of that nonarchaeologist public. Visiting sites with them has dramatically affected my view of myself as an archaeologist, as a scholar, and as an expert. To explain how this happened, I outline how the project unfolded and share many of my experiences in the field in chronological order in the following sections. I finish the chapter by portraying how I have been influenced by the experiences we shared.

THE CONTEXT OF THE PROJECT

The Mesa Verde Project that led to this book began over coffee one morning in the fall of 2009. David Taylor and I care deeply about many of the same issues, which include the state of the environment globally and locally and the state of scholarship and education in the United States. This project has prompted me to ask time and again, "What is a

Why we teach and learn. Students and colleagues at our UNT event in 2012.

university?" My belief is that state-funded universities are currently "eating their young." Bureaucracies are growing, faculty are asked to do more administrative tasks each year, evaluative tools are put in place at an increasing frequency so that English or geography or philosophy can justify their existence in scholarly communities and to politicians. Indeed, my belief extends toward the notion that scholarship is being eroded in American society because learning must now be validated in terms of "return on investment" (ROI). We must now anticipate the benefit of creativity prior to being creative, which makes no sense at all, as creativity is best cooked rare. We should step back and consider, "What would society be like with less artwork, with fewer poets, with fewer opportunities to philosophize?"

Simply asking the question, however, does not diminish my impression that erosion is occurring at an alarmingly rapid rate. The fallout is that academic programs are under intense scrutiny, many are shrinking, and some are being lost. The world is getting crowded, and resources are scarce; stress and strain are ever present. It is in this context that David and I began our conversation; we asked, "What are we passionate about?" This question seems trite, but in the everyday hubbub that has become academia, taking the time to ask it and reflect on it is scary, sad, and hopeful. The answer: we want to work together for the sake of strengthening our senses of scholarly community. Our ROI is that we would likely enjoy our scholarship more because working together would challenge us (now) in new ways. How might we become challenged? Is it a waste of time for artists, poets, filmmakers, scientists, philosophers, and Native persons to go into the field together to learn and to share, with no other stated purpose?

A PHILOSOPHER, AN ARCHAEOLOGIST, A POET, A NATIVE AMERICAN SCHOLAR, A FILMMAKER, AND A PHOTOGRAPHER WALK INTO A BAR . . .

Our work began as a discussion group that focused on creativity and research as storytelling. Each of us tells stories through a lens of the field we occupy, and we legitimize our scholarship in different ways. What leads to a good poem, film, or landscape photograph among those who practice such crafts is different from what legitimizes a research paper in archaeology. Our stated goal from the start has been to share the tools of our crafts, so that we can make scholarship more relevant.

For example, if I (an archaeologist) can learn what the communication devices are for storytelling in landscape photography, I might come to understand different aspects of past and present environments. If I can learn some basic concepts of documentary filmmaking, might I communicate the results of my own research better? The answer is yes, but it turns out (of course) that I am not a poet, nor do I know how to make a film. I cannot offer the traditional knowledge underlying the heritage of Mesa Verde archaeology that a Pueblo person can, and I am not very good at photography. There are all kinds of logical fallacies to the arguments I make because I am not trained in philosophy. Yikes! So, if stories of archaeology, of universities, of human environments, of heritage are to be told through multiple lenses, it must be a cooperative effort. To do so means that I must embark on a journey that is humbling in a world of scholarship that rewards ego.

So we entered this cooperative project together; in Old West fashion (metaphorically speaking), we walked into a bar, circled each other warily for a time, hunkered over our whiskies in isolation, realized we had no stated aim other than to be in the bar together, and began our conversation. I started from a position of distrust, yearning for a more trustful world, community. Can I trust the philosopher (Rob) or the poet (David) not to deconstruct me or my work? Will the photographer (Steve B.) appreciate the research story I tell? What will the award-winning filmmaker (Melinda) in the room think of each of us? She is, after all, "award winning." Does the Native Pueblo person (Porter) take the project seriously? Does his Nativeness make me exotic? Does he think I am simply seeking to benefit professionally on the back of his heritage? Is he *our* Native person? Boundaries firm and steady, we sit at different tables in the bar, but our heads are no longer down or hidden under the brims of the hats of our disciplines and cultures. The fact is, in the current world of academia, reputations are built and careers are made successful through increasingly desperate channels; our distrust is appropriate, and it is a relief to open up.

Sitting at the Same Table

"Why are we here?" "Let's work together." "How?" "Why would we do that when there is no reward for it?" The answer for me: "Something is missing from the scholarship I do." "I am not interested in chasing the same carrot again." "The ROI expected of me from society and the university is not very rewarding personally." "My scholarship is isolated."

Team: "What should we work on together?" Rob: "All research begins in the field." Someone: "Let's go to the field together and see what happens." Me: "I work in the Mesa Verde region; perhaps we could approach the archaeology of that region together and see what happens." We walk out of the bar together. My impression is that each team member wonders what they have gotten into. The guy in front right now happens to be me, an archaeologist. "Does this mean the project is about archaeology?" I think not. It is about entering the field together; archaeology is just a context. Let's move forward. Seriously?!

We were fortunate then that the Center for the Study of Interdisciplinarity (CSID) existed at the University of North Texas. At the time we embarked on our journey, we needed money to sojourn to Mesa Verde. CSID funded two trips, panels at conferences, and eventually a workshop at UNT. We planned a trip to Mesa Verde in July 2011; life intervened, and only four members of the team made that trip. However, we spent months preparing for fieldwork together. It started with a classroom lesson on southwestern archaeology with a focus on the empirical archaeological record of the Mesa Verde region. Thus, the first formal presentation to the group came from me. I took a "just the facts, ma'am" approach, only later to acknowledge that "facts" are relative. Nonetheless, we achieved a starting point, which was followed by presentations about how poets do poetry, how filmmakers make films, how photographers photograph, how philosophers philosophize. Porter Swentzell, from Santa Clara Pueblo, entered the team midstream, as it became clear that we were going to a place that embodies a deep Puebloan heritage.

I semisubconsciously avoided the prospect of bringing a Native person aboard at first, frankly, because it felt inconvenient to me. Archaeologists and Native Americans in the United States are at times at odds, and I had never attempted to work closely with a Pueblo person. Other archaeologists and members of the team pointed out, however, that our inductive, open-ended approach required a team member with expertise in traditional Pueblo knowledge. This was an early hurdle for me: in the company of others, I could not hide and I could not control the research design fully. In response to this challenge, I ended up in contact with Porter. I let go, something I would become accustomed to in the field with the team. It turned out that conscious letting go of the spotlight, of the archaeological story, of control of the direction of the team would be my most important series of contributions. This simple process made me confront, time and again, why it is that I do archaeology. Why am I fascinated with the archaeology of the Pueblo world when it is not my heritage but theirs? I began to ask this question because Rob, the environmental philosopher, was asking it of archaeologists in general. That I am an archaeologist would progressively diminish in importance as our fieldwork took place. "I *am* an archaeologist" is where I started; onion layers began to peal.

MESA VERDE DAYS

Fieldwork was intense; we traveled together for four days in my minivan throughout the Mesa Verde region. Our first visit was to Sand Canyon Pueblo in southwestern Colorado, a place that has inspired my archaeology in a hauntingly deep way since I was a graduate student at the University of Missouri in the 1990s. The place is beautiful. We entered the site, and I told the archaeological story of the occupation of Sand Canyon and how it fits into the regional context of cultural history to the best of my knowledge. Sand Canyon was one of the latest-occupied sites prior to when people left the region at about AD 1300.

Archaeologists characterize the abandonment of Mesa Verde as a period of collapse; there are competing ideas about how the process unfolded that archaeologists debate emphatically. Was regional abandonment the result of deteriorating climate? Was it due to soil depletion from

Steve Wolverton elaborates on the interpretive sign for David Taylor at
Sand Canyon.

intense farming for centuries leading up to the end? A combination of
both? There are many ways that archaeologists write this story that dif-
fer in precise details. My version of the story focuses on a belief that villages moved to locations on the landscape that were defensive, such as cliff
alcoves and canyon heads where water and people could be protected. I
see cloistering into localities on the landscape. Porter would portray a different story. For starters, he would never consider these sites "abandoned."

    I finished my thoughts, and he began (in his disarming and intelli-
gent way) to convey his thoughts. Porter began, "It is always interesting to

me that when archaeologists visit sites, they look down, and when Pueblo people visit sites, they look around." "Perhaps," he conveyed, "people left because it was time to leave." To paraphrase Porter, Pueblos are located in places that have meaning on the landscape, and what he saw at Sand Canyon was disintegration within the village: "We would never organize our villages like this. It seems that you have one group over in this part of the site and another over here." To Porter there appeared to be division within Sand Canyon, which led him to discuss part of his Pueblo world-view in which when humans and culture are out of balance in the world, they must reset their culture, perhaps even by relocating to set a new path. He claimed, "Perhaps these people left because it was time to leave; perhaps it was time to rebalance." Porter and I finished our thoughts at Sand Canyon, and we walked up the trail together; along the way he would pick newly grown piñon-pine needles and lightly chew on them. He suggested that I try it, and the taste was mild and citrus-like. He talked of how when he was little, he and his siblings would try to find the piñon with the best needles. We left David and Steve B. behind at the site to contemplate Sand Canyon through their lenses (really, it began this way: "David, we'll leave you alone to do your poetry"), and I had the pleasure of having my first private conversation with Porter.

Broadly, we discussed the state of the world; he asserted that Pueblo people are part of the world and responsible for it as well as their own culture. For the first time, I was to hear him state that it is the Pueblo way to seek to find the means to become better and better humans. As relatively young men, he explained, there is no way each of us could yet have enough experience to fully address becoming human; however, that ability would grow with experience, he assured me. The downside of seeking to be compassionate, that is, to be a better human being, during one's lifetime is that there is no immediate ROI. How would one measure the impact of kindness? I was increasingly becoming aware that the goals of modern higher education and scholarly research, the goals of ROI, were not necessarily concerned with compassion for global society and human enrichment. Yet the bridge between Porter and me that formed at the picnic table at the head of the trail to Sand Canyon represents what my friend and reputable ecological anthropologist Eugene Anderson terms a "horizontal tie" across the traditional boundaries of culture. I was not studying Porter, and he was not studying me; we were sharing human experience.

Steve Wolverton walks with Porter Swentzell on the top rim at Butler Wash.

BUTLER WASH

During our first field trip, we visited a number of sites, but I remember our site visit to Butler Wash Ruin southwest of Blanding, Utah, vividly. During the summer of 1991, I visited a number of archaeological sites in the American Southwest on a road trip with my father. We were ostensibly celebrating my graduation from high school the previous year, but I think perhaps my father was celebrating his first year as an empty nester. Butler Wash was memorable in that it is a small cliff dwelling situated in a striking red-and-white sandstone landscape. I remember being perched on a cliff above the dwelling, imagining how people used handholds and footholds to scale their way in and out of the small community some 750 years earlier. I already planned to be an archaeologist, but Butler Wash entranced me with the American Southwest. It is where I became fascinated with someone else's heritage, that of the Pueblo peoples. Thinking back, perhaps Pueblo culture was so riveting to me then because I was so dissatisfied with American culture in general. I *gravitated* in this direction, as the days of this period of my youth were hazy with hormones, new experiences, schoolwork, and friends; that is, I am not sure that engaging archaeology was a conscious choice so much as a series of steps echoing C. S. Lewis's "further up, further in." Eventually, I simply *was* an archaeologist.

As my university education progressed, I came to view American history as ethnocentric, and though the United States promotes democracy and individual freedom, its culture seemed to do so at the expense of common decency and human dignity at times. This is a harsh judgment that is personally biased, but it represented my state of mind then. The attraction to a different history was more than fascinating; it was a refuge.

Importantly, I did not know much about Pueblo culture, and I still do not. I studied material culture, particularly animal bones from the past. I had returned to Butler Wash in 2009 with my wife, Lisa, and my son, Peter, for the first time in decades; it was no less impressive. In 2011 it was a genuine pleasure to arrive at the site with Steve B., Porter, and David. There, Porter and I wandered the landscape together; we headed north above the cliff dwelling, seeking to reach the horizon of the mesa above Butler Wash. We kept finding new horizons and eventually turned back. Steve B. crafted one of his first large panoramic landscape pieces at Butler Wash, and David delved deeply into Porter's description of pictographs near the site. It was during this visit that Porter first encouraged us to simply sit and to experience the place quietly. Later, he would voice this as "Your culture has it almost completely backward, seeking knowledge before respect; sit there and watch, listen, have respect before knowledge, and then you might understand a bit about a place." This advice will stick with me for the rest of my life; as an archaeologist, the temptation is to delve into a site, to generate data, knowledge, and then from that process one learns. Porter was asking for us to do the opposite.

ASTROFALFA

We've just visited Edge of the Cedars and Butler Wash Ruin together, beautiful and inspiring places, and we drive home the southern route past Hatch Trading Post, briefly wandering through Hovenweep. It has been a long day, and Hovenweep was hot! The group seems tired of visiting sites, and we have more places to go tomorrow. To me, these places are poetic and these landscapes are majestic. It disturbs me to hear David state in a stressful tone, "I do not really know what I am doing here."

I would react to David's statement for some time, responding to it in one of the CSID blog posts that I wrote, "Synergy First: An Interdisciplinary Story." I constantly appraised my role on the team during those early months, especially in the field. The project put *working together about stories* above aims and goals. David's frustration was justified; we could not anticipate ROI. I felt that I was becoming the team's glue; it became my job to suspend opinion, to suspend archaeology, to "go all in" without requiring a systematic goal. That day I committed fully to our team's inductive flavor; this work was about experiential threads of creative minds exploring the Mesa Verde landscape together. The project was to increasingly become a panacea for frustration with overly tailored academia, so-called bean counting related to enrollment numbers, student retention, "customer service," and (of course) the now fully detested ROI. I would later write, on September 14, 2011, about how this type of commitment feels:

> Research is a creative enterprise, and speaking for myself, creative expression provides a handle on an unpredictable world. What I am referring to are waxing and waning financial markets, pulses of political instability and social tragedy, increasingly visible media portrayal of natural disasters, local university budgetary facts of life, students with similarly pulsating states of emergency. What is it about the cooperative enterprise of our team that resonates with a sense of satisfaction and tranquility? Frankly, I *get* to be a part of something creative, that is immediate, that is shared, and that builds ties with others telling similar and different stories. This cooperative, creative process feels productive without endpoints. "Projected endpoints . . ."; these represent the usual state of things. In contrast, our team must be built on trust because the endpoints will be poems that I cannot write, films that I cannot make, photographs that I cannot take, and knowledge that I only have a small portion of.
>
> Process. Is this a key to interdisciplinarity? Or is *process* a personal window to the world of research and nothing more?

Later, as we began to present "Mesa Verde Stories," scholars would question whether our team was multi-, inter-, or transdisciplinary. Were we working alongside each other independently and then converging later, or were we working together in the field and back home, or do our products transcend individual disciplines entirely? Scholarly members of our audience were looking for discrete products, perhaps poems written by the poet, the filmmaker, and the archaeologist. Or perhaps a film by the filmmaker, the philosopher, the photographer, and the Tewa person. But the process underlying our poetry, film, photography, that is, the shared experience, is more important.

Do we ever really leave our individualism behind? As David would point out in our presentation to the public in Denton, Texas, in March 2012, "Steve B.'s photography may seem independent of my poetry, Porter's Tewa knowledge, Rob's philosophy, and Melinda's film, but look more closely. There is a thread throughout. In the panoramic of Butler Wash Ruin, Steve W. and Porter are there walking toward the horizon, and there I am writing the poetry displayed on the same walls as Steve B.'s photography and Melinda's film." Rob and Melinda would infuse this place with their own stories on our second visit, in October 2011. David's thread through all of our work stemmed from the fact that we went to the field together. I was shocked and pleasantly surprised at how much things had changed for him since that day in July on the way back from Hovenweep, when he wondered what he was doing in my minivan, visiting these sites.

That day, as we ascended out of Hovenweep country back toward the Dolores River valley, we became "the Four Amigos." We drove through alfalfa fields growing in the desert, watered from the Colorado River, which no longer flows to the Gulf of California. It is spent by its "stake-holders" long before Mexicans receive the downstream effects (no water) of those using the river in the United States. Porter acknowledged how fake it is to grow alfalfa in the high desert: "We should just replace these artificially green fields with synthetic alfalfa; it would be just as produc-tive." He coined the term *astrofalfa*, which we would guffaw over for miles and months. We were *clever*, but inside I know that our laughter concerned something deeper.

We are dissatisfied in our powerlessness. If water conservation and environmental ethics were of central concern, then the most impor-tant stakeholder on the Colorado River would be Mexico. If down-stream effects were put first, then the precautionary principle to "first do no harm" would be in place. Political ecology, the intermixing of econ-omy, society, politics, and environmental policy, however, is a reality. We sat in the Dolores River Brewpub that evening, laughing over this ridic-ulous product, astrofalfa, that we had invented in our minds. We looked longingly out the window, across the street at an old ski chalet that is in a constant state of renovation. Someone said, "That would make a great university; let's just start our own. We'll call it Astrofalfa Univer-sity, AU, or Hey You, or Hay You!" We would model our university, per-haps, after Quest University in Canada, where students center their entire

Yucca Mountain peeking over the horizon at Goodman Point.

curriculum on questions they have about the world. I love the memory of our laughter and our camaraderie, which would never have happened if we had not embarked into the field together. But bitterness underlies that laughter still; I rest firm in my belief that if we are to improve environmental ethics, we must become Aldo Leopold's "plain citizens of nature." We must be fascinated by outdoor places.

It is tempting, for purposes of ROI, to study stuff at the expense of going places and being there. Fieldwork together from wildly different scholarly perspectives cracked that code. We walked into a bar together.

Frozen Stories
The entire team entered the field together on October 5, 2011. This time we would tackle Mesa Verde National Park. Cold weather came early that fall, and temperatures at night fell into the low twenties. By the time we arrived at MVNP, I had a clear sense of my role on the team as "quiet facilitator." My friends are not prima donnas; they do not require much. However, they are noted scholars attempting to cross comfort zones that are narrowed and solidified in the bean-counting environments of academic ROI. There is no reward, other than experience, for open-ended

inductive fieldwork with scholars outside of one's home discipline. I assumed (correctly or not) that this process would not feel comfortable. So, with as much effort as I could muster, I quietly ran circles around the group, trying to account for every detail of organization, management, comfort. As Melinda would state, in film terms, I was the producer of the project.

The moniker *Producer* put a label on what I felt my role to be. I was worried, and here's an example of why. Melinda makes excellent films about environmental issues, films about rivers, ranching, death. She's good at it. So here we sit at the Morefield Campground at MVNP. It's cold. I feel responsible, as I now feel that I have convinced a lifelong friend (Steve B.), an internationally known scholar of environmental justice issues (Rob), a kind, intelligent, and dedicated Pueblo person (Porter), a doubting poet (David), and an award-winning filmmaker to visit the Mesa Verde region together as an experiment in induction. There is no doubt that I was dramatizing at the time because these colleagues chose to embark on this adventure, but this vignette is not about the truth; it's about how I felt. So far, our only "product"? Astrofalfa. And two of our team members (Rob and Melinda) did not take part in the etymology of the concept.

And so I worked at it. Archaeology was suspended as much as ever. This fieldwork was to be about their visits to sites and places in the region. Weather cooperating, we might capture meaningful footage and experiences. Together, we did all that we could to account for the cold: Wal-Mart in Cortez provided heat packets for our socks; beer and cigars around the campfire kept us going. By night we shivered in the freezing rain, sleet, and snow. Rob slept poorly, and at least one of us (not Melinda) snored loudly. This trip, however, was to greatly expand our shared experience about stories in the field. We were able to encounter and contemplate the place of Mesa Verde and the role of archaeology in the park intensely based on our visits.

During the first half of the trip, we had to throw out our proposed itinerary, as the weather was too wet and cold at MVNP for filming. We revisited Butler Wash Ruin with the whole team. The experience was wholly different from previous visits; Rob and Porter wandered across the mesa together, and Melinda dove into filming the landscape. Lighting did not permit good conditions for filming the cliff dwelling, so Melinda, David, and Porter would make another trip to Butler Wash that week. At some point early in the week, we also visited with archaeologists at Crow

Our group (minus Steve Bardolph) considering the clouds on the rim above Butler Wash.

Canyon. A spontaneous dialogue about archaeologists, cultural heritage, and stories ensued. I did not anticipate how exposed archaeologists would be to the lenses of poetry, filmmaking, philosophy, and art; I also did not anticipate how open archaeologists would be to a dialogue that was increasingly focusing on who owns the story of the past.

The team was now taking on a life of its own. A solidity of purpose was evolving centered on a couple of themes. Rob, for example, throughout the team's history, but vividly on this trip, would infuse dialogue with targeted questions about cross-cultural respect for heritage. I did not underestimate at the time, nor do I now, how important Rob was to the team. He consistently raised a mirror to our American selves, to my archaeologist self. So a central theme of heritage evolved from Rob's presence in the group. As the trip progressed, I would phrase this theme around the question "Who owns the story?" In addition, I came to realize that there was no single story about Mesa Verde Pueblo archaeology, and as a result poets and photographers had no more or less to say than archaeologists and Pueblo peoples.

Importantly, there are power dynamics as to who owns the story of the past at Mesa Verde. Archaeologists study material remains in great detail with intense focus, and this provides some important information and some ownership. But the heritage of the place belongs to modern Native Americans, especially Pueblo people. So, could we do the story of Mesa Verde heritage any justice through our various lenses? This question ended up being irrelevant, because our team members were not attracted to telling the cultural stories embedded in the place of Mesa Verde. To paraphrase Rob, "Any one of us can claim this story about Mesa Verde heritage, but we will still eat sushi in Cortez tonight." We like our convenient lives, and we often claim a heritage only at our own convenience. Increasingly, a second theme emerged: we began to tell the stories of our experiences together in this place, at this time, wrapped in Pueblo heritage, at a distance from the "facts" of archaeology.

The team split up for periods to cover ground, and we reconvened at Spruce Tree House one late afternoon and evening. We observed that different stories about the abandonment of the cliff dwellings are told to different audiences and by different storytellers. A chronicle of interactions at Spruce Tree House is as follows. During the visit, Melinda was filming, audio was being recorded, Steve B. was photographing, and other members were simply interacting and listening. The rangers had a certain story they would tell the general public. They would point out different architectural features of the village, and depending on the questions asked by tourists they would dive into questions about prehistoric life at Spruce Tree House leading up to abandonment. Their stories varied with the questions asked, but generally aligned with archaeological interpretations. They were the "experts"; tourists were the "students." In this context, we (the filmmaker, photographer, poet, and others) were all "nonexperts"; the rangers were storytellers. There were clear spatial boundaries; members of the team were not allowed to enter private areas of the site and were kept behind chains for tourists.

The same boundaries existed for a private tour guide who led a group through; in this case, he was clearly the storyteller, and his audience deferred to him and largely ignored the rangers. Spatial boundaries were the same as for the team members. Dominos fell. Porter's last name is well known in the American Southwest. His family members are known by the park staff members, and they are considered Pueblo experts. In addition, there is transparent respect for Native people among the staff. Most versions of their stories about the dwellings that we encountered acknowledged that the descendants of those who lived there still live in the Southwest and continue to view the area as important. Hopi consultants regularly visit the park, for example, and provide insights as to the interpretation of the sites for communication with the general public.

Once the rangers became aware of Porter, his last name, and his Tewa background, he immediately became the expert, and he was the dominant storyteller (by no means did he try to be dominating; people simply listened intently). Spatial boundaries evaporated because Spruce Tree House was *his place*. The story changed once more, and the creative members of our team were able to encounter the site in whole new ways. There was a meshing experience of openness from the rangers and cultural expertise from Porter that greatly enriched the photography, film, poetry, prose—the art, philosophy, and humanities—taking place then and there. Science ceased even further to be the backstory and became mere details.

Interestingly, on a trip to Spruce Tree House in June 2011, I witnessed a similar shift in who was to be considered "expert" when I visited the site with archaeologist Donna Glowacki. Although she was the storyteller, more conservative spatial boundaries existed. That is, she held the story, but not the space. I would find out from Donna later that it is MVNP policy to openly engage members of Pueblo communities. She would tell me about a similar experience she had with young Jemez Pueblo dancers who visited the site while she was documenting architecture there.

BETTER HUMANS

When I was in college at Arizona State University (ASU), the Honors College required a course entitled the Human Event, which focused on literature, philosophy, religion, and metaphysics. Why was this class required? The Honors College professors and administrators at ASU understood that the real purpose of a university is to build better citizenry, which in turn requires that we question our purposes as humans. With this idea in mind, the goal of a university is "respect before knowledge." If one thinks about it, science is designed to do the same. The implicit aim of an education completely determines the flavor of the learning process and outcome. Is there a place for education as service and citizenship in American society today? Our team has forced respect before knowledge upon ourselves, which flies in the face of a system that requires one to anticipate ROI prior to engaging in scholarship. It did not matter at the start that we chose to focus on Mesa Verde archaeology, which was simply a place to go. It mattered that we went together. Hindsight is 20/20; we were fortunate that we chose Mesa Verde, because it brought Porter to our team and the archaeology of the region is imbued with deep questions about humanity and storytelling. Make no mistake, Porter is part of our team; he is not simply a convenient regional add-on. Though we might travel to North Texas, Argentina, China, or Europe to study culture and environment, if he desires, he will be part of it because he brings respect before knowledge.

In a sense, addressing fieldwork in this manner has leveled the playing field of academia. Am I an archaeologist first? Am I a professor first? A father, friend, colleague, (dare I say) poet? Is your DNA sequence more important than David's poem? Does your knowledge of market forces trump my knowledge of material culture? Is your philosophy of pedagogy more important than Rob's penetrating questions about environmental justice? Does your 3-D image of a carbon nanotube outshine Melinda's eight-minute sound-saturated film or Steve B.'s panoramic artwork? Is my heritage of individualism more important than Porter's to become a better human being? You'll find out if you do what we did.

As an Archaeologist, What Next?

When I talk about the *Sushi in Cortez* project with other colleagues, they want to know what the product is or will be. Despite the fact that our group has explicitly sought to avoid ROI and to place a premium on inductive, creative interdisciplinarity in the field, questions pervade about the productivity of this research. I know that this project will not lead to a new publication by me in the *Journal of Archaeological Science, American Antiquity*, or the *Journal of Archaeological Method and Theory*. In fact, dressing this research up in such a manner would be rather disingenuous and would, thus, represent a failure of the project, because this book and this team have never been about "doing archaeology." So what's the point? This

Steve Wolverton talks with the shadow of Steve Bardolph at Hovenweep.

project has already led to new films, poems, and teaching styles for other members of the team. Readers may surmise that I have simply tagged along for the ride; nothing could be further from the truth. This project has changed my perspective on what it means to be an archaeologist and a scholar.

I chose to become an archaeologist because I found the study of the human past through the medium of material culture to be fascinating. The process of touching, viewing, and encountering tools, buildings, bones, and other artifacts is fascinating to me because I can imagine what the past was like more vividly. For example, when I visit Sand Canyon

Pueblo and walk through the now silent open plazas, I imagine families there, children playing, conflict, food processing, and the comings and goings of past cultures. I feel that I am part of it. However, as my career has progressed, that sense of fascination has ceased to be enough to fuel my research agenda. Over my career, particularly the past decade, my curiosity has waned. Signs of this include a shift toward "applied zooarchaeological" research as one of my specialties. In this line of work, researchers employ zooarchaeological data on the animal remains recovered from archaeological sites for determining benchmarks for conservation biology. Briefly, applied zooarchaeologists answer questions such as the following: What animals were common in an area in the past? Should certain species be considered native to an area or not? What types of interactions have humans had with particular animal species over time? The answers to these questions have important meaning for conservation biology, which seeks to sustain the continued evolution of biodiversity on an increasingly human-impacted and crowded earth. This avenue of research is inherently interdisciplinary, another pathway of my more recent scholarship. Applied research and interdisciplinarity encourage my curiosity, something progressively more difficult in "pure" archaeology and zooarchaeology. Why?

I hesitate to answer this question for fear that I will seem self-centered, but the short answer is that my archaeological research was becoming less and less about subject matter and increasingly about particularistic arguments and debates. Learning to navigate the worlds of peer review, grant writing, and subdisciplinary politics is akin to learning to play chess. There are plans and strategies involved that center on what to say, when to say it, how to convey narrative, when to publish, and (if one is lucky enough) when to secure grant funding. I learned to play that professional game well enough to receive tenure, and I reached a level of achievement that exceeded my own expectations. That said, archaeology has come to mean playing the game to such an extent that my original, youthful, and creative sense of fascination has wavered. Am I experiencing claustrophobia in archaeology? Becoming applied and interdisciplinary has provided a new sense of freedom and a new audience.

My question of "Why interdisciplinarity?" has not been fully answered, however. I find a separate aspect of archaeology frustrating, the precept that "archaeology is anthropological or it is nothing." For me, archaeology is *archaeological* or it is nothing. Archaeology is anthropological because it concerns the material culture left by humans, but it has never made sense to me to consider the objects and residues of past material culture as direct data sources on past human behaviors. I have never desired to reconstruct past cultures and behaviors via the study of artifacts, architecture, refuse, and so forth—those remain mysteriously imaginary and inspiring.

I am content to understand the past distributions of animal species, what species were hunted, whether or not particular species declined or increased over time in abundance, where people lived or did not, and other relatively simple topics. Certainly, these offer some information concerning how people behaved, but I find that many other archaeologists desire to understand past cultures in much fuller detail. Their fascination with such detail is rewarded in archaeology; in contrast, my stoic empiricism is considered bland and unappealing. I could attempt to rewrite archaeology in my own terms, but I have no desire to do so. Further, it would fall on deaf ears. I am quite satisfied with my bland, empirical works because embedded within them are my full confidence and awe that the past remains a mystery. These days, I simply wish to encounter that sense of mystery in new ways.

To debate whether I think archaeology is anthropological is to navigate dangerous political waters for multiple reasons. When Lewis Binford and Walter W. Taylor pushed hard for archaeology as anthropology in the 1950s and 1960s, what did they mean? They really meant archaeology as cultural anthropology. That is, the intended product of archaeology should be less descriptive and something more fleshed out, such as ethnography. During the same period, Binford in particular pushed hard to make archaeology scientific. We were to be scientific *and* anthropological. I will not digress into defining science, but for my archaeological colleagues, I agree with the late archaeologist Robert Dunnell's summary of archaeology as anthropology/science published in several papers in the 1970s and 1980s. Throughout my career, I have settled comfortably into what many archaeologists describe as Dunnell's "sterile physics of artifacts." Simply put, this type of archaeology is labeled as sterile because Dunnell considered it a study of objects first and of behavior only indirectly—if at all. Heated and sometimes vitriolic published debates have developed in archaeology over what archaeology should be. Working with this interdisciplinary group, however, solidified for me that archaeology is not akin to cultural anthropology in a roundabout manner.

If we are anthropological, we should adopt one of the foundational principles of anthropology, that of cultural relativism, which broadly means that one cannot understand a separate culture unless one becomes part of it. There are ethical boundaries concerning cultural appropriation that anthropologists have learned are important over the past century. One should not use knowledge about another culture for professional gain if harm comes to the people who are being studied. Some might argue that even the act of making someone or a group of people a subject initiates oppression. There is quite a bit of gray area, but in general cultural anthropologists are concerned about the people they work with.

In the Mesa Verde region, archaeologists study Ancestral Pueblo culture, and during the process we interact with modern Pueblo people who do not want us to excavate Pueblo sites. Our goals concerning the study of the past are anthropological, but when confronted with this challenge we may shape-shift away from anthropology to science. Many archaeologists listen to Pueblo people and adjust their research agendas to respect cultural boundaries, but when we do not it is often because we claim that the goals of science, or the need to critically examine and learn from the past for the betterment of humanity as a whole, are most important. And they are, except that by so doing we bump up against an inability to practice cultural relativism. If we ask what members of another culture are concerned about as human beings, and if their concerns conflict with the anthropological goals of archaeology, what is to be done? Is there a scientific goal of archaeology that is more important than being anthropological? It is interesting to watch the ease with which my nonarchaeological colleagues show respect for Porter's cultural heritage. Clearly, he would prefer that archaeologists not excavate Ancient Pueblo sites; his perspective matters to them *first* because they consider him an equal *partner* in an interdisciplinary project. They do not bring the political baggage of "being an archaeologist" to the team, they do not have a preconceived research agenda with default goals that conflict with Porter's heritage, and they do not put archaeology first because they are not archaeologists. This new category of peer pressure is glorious and liberating. Frankly, I like it, but it leaves me a little confused as to what I will do next within archaeology.

Unequivocally, archaeologists *do* have many answers to questions about the human past because we are the ones who study it intensely, but I am skeptical of our resolution. Take Mesa Verde abandonment as an example. There is a definite problem of equifinality (multiple potential causes leading to the same outcome) in our long arguments about cultural change at AD 1300 in the region. Some archaeologists lean toward deteriorating environment as a hallmark cause; others claim overpopulation and all of the problems that accompany it. Some argue for conflict, warfare, and even cannibalism. Porter told me that perhaps people left because *they chose to*. "Maybe it was time for them to leave, and they knew it" (to paraphrase him). A product of this project for me is a newfound belief that archaeologists should look outward to the public, to other scholars, and to those people most affected by the outcomes of our research (for example, Native Americans) for the questions they have about our conclusions. We should do this as least as much as (if not more than) we present our results, discussion, and conclusions to other archaeologists. Such nonexperts represent challenging audiences to convince about our stories.

More important, however, is that I am now uncomfortable with doing archaeological research in the American Southwest. I have not quit doing research there, but I am more wary of how I engage in the entire research process. I can share two short stories that exemplify why I feel this way. First, I lead a team of researchers that has had substantial support from the National Science Foundation to develop improved methods for extracting protein food residues from prehistoric cooking pottery. The implications of this research are extensive for archaeological chemistry, but the most compelling research product has been personal. In the process of groundtruthing our method, we encountered a human intestinal cell protein residue from an abandonment-context potsherd from the Mesa Verde region. This is not the type of protein that would inadvertently be found as a contaminant in a lab; I have read grand stories written about cannibalism and other topics based on poorer-quality residue analyses, and believe me the temptation was there to write a highly publishable story! However, working with Porter and with the Crow Canyon Archaeological Center (as well as because I have a heart that is only one or two sizes too small), I decided not to pursue those stories but instead to engage people from modern Pueblos and archaeologists at Crow Canyon about how to proceed. At first I felt like a drug addict turning my stash over to the police, knowing it was the best in the long term but feeling the pang of letting go of a sure short-term gain; that is, it was an emotionally trying decision not to put science first (later it turned out not to matter anyway).

I approached the Native American Advisory Group at Crow Canyon Archaeological Center (through which the excavations had been

Spiraling. Corrugated cooking pot base from Goodman Point.

administered) and notified them of the potential result. Critical reexamination and replication of the work *did not validate the result*. However, in the process of revealing the preliminary result to the Advisory Group, several issues surfaced. First, members of the group were genuinely upset that human remains of any kind had been excavated and analyzed (even though they understood that such analysis was unintended, preliminary, and unverified). Second, they wanted all residue analysis to stop until a new course of action could be recommended. They did encourage us to validate our initial result, which we were unable to do. Coincidentally, this all played out during the same period as the field research for this book. There were times during the fieldwork that I felt I was horribly hypocritical for not sharing the implications of the residue research I am part of, but I kept quiet as too much had already been done without full consultation with the Advisory Group.

I was relieved that we were unable to validate the result because, although it would have been immanently publishable, it would also have been unavoidably insulting to members of the Advisory Group to publish the results (and whatever story we would choose to convey as experts). During the validation process, I met via conference call with the Advisory Group, and I decided to open the books on our lab process, to share all that we do, and to convey in detail our approach. I found myself wanting "them" to know all about what "we" were doing. And by so doing, I gave them complete discretion to "pull the plug" on our residue analysis of Ancient Pueblo potsherds. They did not pull the plug, but I believe they were empowered by being on the inside of the research. I should have asked their opinions (a definite plural because members of the group do not always agree) prior to proposing and beginning the research.

Why didn't I? Frankly, encountering human residues never seemed within the scope of possibility. Crow Canyon diligently avoids excavation of human burials and, as a result of our preliminary result, has revised their human-remains policy to account for bioanalytical residue analysis, an important outcome. However, the real lesson for archaeologists is that we often *don't ask so that we cannot be told no*, an archaeological sin that I am increasingly aware of in my own work. As archaeologists, our work is not trivial and has real-world impacts on living, breathing human beings. Being "archaeological" or "scientific," though valuable, does not trump being human. Other archaeologists may be versed in this, but for me it was new.

The second story concerns a short visit to my lab with Porter Swentzell when he came to Denton for the interdisciplinary display and panel in the spring of 2012. I always believed that I had escaped the political and social conflicts related to analysis of human skeletal remains by studying zooarchaeology, which is research on animal remains. I am quite proud of our zooarchaeology lab facility at UNT. It's modern and has a fume hood, a passable reference collection, and retractable outlets that hang from the ceiling (the brilliant idea of my wife and fellow zooarchaeologist, Lisa Nagaoka). When I showed Porter around the lab, I shared with him the projects that we had been working on. One of the collections of remains that I shared even has a hawk burial. I recognized immediately that Porter was taken aback, and I asked why. He respectfully conveyed that some people (his people) believe that animals are nonhuman persons (a term I first encountered from friend and colleague Eugene Anderson, an ethnobiologist, the same person mentioned earlier in the chapter concerning horizontal ties). To paraphrase Porter, "When that animal was laid to rest, it was out of some respect and for an important reason, which is every bit as important as when humans are laid to rest." Those may not have been his exact words, but that's what I recall.

There are archaeologists who offer the valid argument that past behaviors may have been very different and that Porter's perspective may not apply to the past. However, when anthropologists study living non-Western cultures, we often encounter beliefs that make no sense to us that can be invalidated when considered from the perspective of Western science. The important point is that Porter feels and lives this connection between the past and the present, and his claim cannot be invalidated. I find it difficult in this situation to be anthropological and scientific at the same time, and I find it nearly impossible to fully respect Porter's cultural heritage while also pursuing zooarchaeological analysis of the hawk burial. The issue is not one of "Who is correct about the past?" The issue is one of how to determine appropriate cross-cultural boundaries that are fair—respect before knowledge. I am left wondering, "What will I do with these remains, where should I send them as it's an orphan collection, and what are my responsibilities?" I am still not certain.

Here's what I am certain of. I cannot pretend that my experience with the members of this team, with Porter in particular, and with the Native American Advisory Group did not happen. I regard my research as archaeological and scientific, both of which are interesting and important. However, I no longer remain naive to the fact that there are political and social implications surrounding and embedded in the research that I do, no matter how small those implications might seem to me. At some level, I am bashful about the nature of this interdisciplinary research and its implications for my career. "What will others think? Will I be dismissed? Will others listen?" In the end, each scholar must navigate the ethical implications of their own research, and whether a person chooses to attempt to "be a better human being" in the process is really none of my business. I move forward within this interdisciplinary team and outside of it, feeling fortunate to study archaeology for the rich sense of curiosity it allows me.

2

Spinning in Circles

Steve Bardolph

As I write this in mid-March from Duluth, Minnesota, my research friends are on spring break, and I imagine them lounging and chatting in an out-door beer garden in Denton, Texas, enjoying the warm seventy-three-degree evening and the promise of a sunny week in the eighties. I wish I could join them. I'm in the midst of a warm spell too, a whopping thirty-seven degrees, but that will end tonight as we return to snow and twenties for the foreseeable future. So, how did I, a photographer and designer from the frigid North, get connected with the Mesa Verde Stories group, also known as "Equipo de A" or the southern branch of the "A-Team"?

I am fortunate that my archaeologist friend Steve Wolverton doesn't know many photographers. Two years ago, as Steve, the poet, the film-maker, and the philosopher (each outstanding in their fields) were con-sidering a shared trip to the Mesa Verde region, they thought it might be interesting to bring a few more perspectives to the mix. Porter, our Tewa collaborator, was an obvious choice. I was the other. Academics who like to play outside where it's warm. What could be better? I jumped at the oppor-tunity, even though I was in the final throes of my tenure-track probationary period, struggling to play the game well, prove myself, and give 125 per-cent to my research, teaching, and service . . . which oddly meant spending more hours in front of a glowing screen in a dark university basement writ-ing e-mails than anything else. They pulled me out of the dungeon and the morass of my in-box to lend a 360-degree perspective to the fieldwork.

VISUAL AND VERBAL MOSAICS

When I'm not busy with administrivia, I love to share, through immer-sive photographic panoramas, the awe I experience at the flaming, shining

Steve Bardolph head shot with camera (taken into a mirror).

grandeur in the world around me. My goal is to help people see, even in everyday events and places, life charged with deep freshness and bright wonder. These panoramas are my primary artistic and design direction, and I've been exploring the human interaction with beautiful and sublime landscapes for twenty years. These works emulate a Japanese garden, at once presenting an awe-inspiring and complete whole, as well as a lush tapestry of individual details spread across singular moments in time. They ground the viewer in real space while employing a familiar and comfortable grid borrowed from graphic design, yet they break the window of conventional perspective by reaching around and behind to shift points of view and invite an exuberant interaction with place and time.

Bear with me while I share a bit more of the self-aggrandizing tenure-track verbiage, quoted from my tenure application:

> In Bardolph's work, form contributes to narrative. Sense of place is paramount. Structure is applied for problem solving and clarity. Honesty and integrity are valued as much as beauty and organization. Space and time are fractured then reassembled in a dancing mosaic to enhance user experience. In Bardolph's collaborative and interdisciplinary work, grid systems, pattern, and shifting perspectives help to weave and synthesize disparate viewpoints into a compelling story line. What can at first appear playfully simple is rich with contrast, questions, and discoveries. What seems complete can be fragmentary, and what looks shattered may be a unified entity. Behind the clean order and repetition lurk deeper discussions of boundaries, borders, authority, power, ethics, culture, sustainability and spirituality. Typography is used at times to focus and direct interpretation, and in other works stripped away to invite further consideration.

This is more or less true, but anything grand, wonderful, noble, or profound in my work, especially my recent work, I attribute to divine inspiration and the influence and collaboration of my Mesa Verde teammates. Thanks to grants, I have some cool photographic toys, including super-wide-angle lenses, a monster computer, and access to a freakishly wide-format printer.

On my own I have a moth-to-flame attraction to beauty, I love to be outside, and I'm fascinated by space and place. Thanks to an early-childhood education in Germany, I crave order and am comforted by systems, repetition, and ritual. I like fiddling with words on a page. No, that doesn't mean writing. I dread writing and would rather clean gutters, chop ice, change diapers, and file taxes than write. It's the shape and placement of individual letters I enjoy, and I make a profession of it teaching typography. Swirl all that together, and you get panoramas like the ones included in this book.

I have approached this chapter like one of my panoramas, sharing a grab bag of intimate snippets and details, placing them side by side, row by row, round and round, and once finished, with distance and reflection, presenting a coherent whole. This is a written mosaic that includes personal experiences, thoughts, realizations, and interactions with the Mesa Verde group and region that have shaped me as a person and a professor. Whether you find it lazy or innovative, I hope this nonlinear narrative of broken text tiles will assemble into a colorful and informative picture of my interactions with interdisciplinarity and the Ancient Pueblo landscape and how my research, thoughts, and teaching have changed as a result. In the spirit of our team and all the other risks we've taken so far, here goes.

Minnesota versus Texas

When I told my colleagues at the University of Minnesota–Duluth (UMD) about my upcoming interdisciplinary collaboration, it always sounded like Steve W.'s joke from the previous chapter: an archaeologist, a poet, a filmmaker, a Tewa consultant, a philosopher, and I walk into a bar but I didn't yet know the punch line. My Minnesota colleagues were intrigued, looked at me expectantly, and waited for the plan, the overriding theme and research goal. It was a little embarrassing not to have one, so I started pitching something like:

> Together we'll use our diverse scholarly lenses and experience to examine challenging topics in the southwestern United States in order to create broader awareness, lively discussion, and deeper understanding of indigenous populations and sustainability in the academic research community and the public at large. In the Mesa Verde region we'll study the rise, spread, and collapse of an ancient and complex American Pueblo society in southwestern Colorado, southern Utah, northern New Mexico and Arizona in an effort to understand how and why human cultures change over time. We plan to share our findings in exhibitions, conference presentations, short films, and the written word.

Okay, at least I wrote that in grant applications. It sounds dramatic to say "collapse." Turns out, there probably was no collapse; they just moved south. What about the deeper understanding of indigenous populations? Well, maybe, but that's hardly my (or even our) story to tell. Amid some embarrassing discoveries and realizations, we're finding we can only authentically and honestly share our own stories and experience.

In the joke we walk into the bar . . . together. This unity, despite wild diversity, may itself be the biggest payoff for me. Though, of course, there are merits to the bar as well. During my first evening physically with the group, we shared schnitzel, sauerkraut, brats, and beer in a German pub in Cortez, Colorado.

Why not collaborate with my university colleagues in Duluth? We're seemingly too overburdened by politics, by economic and departmental woes, and with all our day-to-day struggles that we might never get around to it, and within Art & Design we may not have the diversity of perspectives to be as interesting. How about other departments at UMD? Good idea, if in a new context, like "in the field." Otherwise, we may only talk shop, strut egos, or talk about the bad weather (since that's what we do in Minnesota, given there's so much of it).

Why collaborate with scholars in Texas? Well, it's a lot more fun. It involves camping, pizza, and beer. Hiking, travel, flight, adventure, some adversity, and, most of all, people I like, who accept and appreciate me for who I am.

When this whole project started, we gathered to present our work in a classroom and via Skype. I was swept away by the research of each team member in turn, head spinning, thoughts dancing, scribbling notes, and increasingly nervous about sharing my own work and story. All these tenured faculty, published authors, and an award-winning filmmaker. So, what did they say after my presentation? Amid the comments and questions, I can still hear Rob, surprised I wasn't tenured already, saying, "Don't worry, your tenure is in the bag." Seldom have I felt such respect at my own institution. I was shocked at the immediate level of trust and bonding. With anxiety rapidly changing to excitement, I remember thinking, "I can't wait to work with these people!"

LETTING GO OF CONTROL

Before each trip into the field, I spent months scouting our intended sites online and figuring out the perfect gear. Maybe this is how my pretrip jitters manifested? I ordered and tested three different photo-expedition backpacks. Whatever I took had to fit as a carry-on, but include everything I might need: big camera and lenses for "serious" work, medium camera for panoramas, backup medium camera, 360 panoramic lens, waterproof camera for inclement conditions, small camera to wear on my belt so I would never miss an unexpected yet decisive moment. Camera phone. Maybe I'm packing too many cameras? Nonsense, there's no such thing as too many cameras. How about a laptop? Will I need a laptop in the field? While hiking? You never know; stick it in. Chargers. Power strip. Batteries. More batteries. Flash cards. Good thing I don't have to carry film anymore. I even purchased a new camera for the second trip, a Canon G12. Blowing sand on the first night of the first trip ruined my Canon G11. See, I should have been carrying a water- and sand-proof camera as well. I bought a new 360 lens and a big CamelBak water bladder for long hikes. Rocket Blaster lens cleaning brush. I packed a half gallon of assorted sunscreens. Long sleeves. Short sleeves. Long pants, shorts, and zip-off pants. Tilley hat. Hiking boots. Hiking shoes. I was living out a photographic excursion fantasy, with all the gear I ever wanted.

I show up looking like a Sherpa, all my techno wizardry stuffed in my fancy, new, expandable LowePro photo backpack with waterproof cover and built-in hydration solution, carrying a hidden MacBook Air laptop on every hike, and David shows up with a bandanna, running shoes, a notebook, and pencil. Steve Wolverton and Porter pack even less, but they have knowledge (and wisdom) of the area. I don't think Rob brought anything at all, save his enormous brain. Thank goodness Melinda has an entire carful of Pelican cases, bags, batteries, rigs, rails, tripods, and sound equipment so I'm not quite so embarrassed, but astoundingly nobody bats an eye.

My first photographs and panoramas in Colorado at Sand Canyon and Goodman Point bombed. Was it the weather? Did I have too specific a goal or previsualization? Bad equipment? Was I just getting warmed up? Poor lighting? Not yet in the groove or connected to the group? Maybe it's that when we got to our first archeological site, all I saw were clumps of bushes and some scattered rock piles. Echoes of Monty Python rattled in my brain: "We bring you a shrubbery!" Not until I got out onto a small cliff edge could I intuitively understand why an ancient people might live there. Good breeze coming up the canyon, a trickle of water from the slope above, green trees all around, the sturdy stone embrace of the canyon itself, and a southern exposure that led to a grand view of distant

Steve Bardolph hiking around Butler Wash site. Photograph by Rob Figueroa.

Yucca Mountain (known to many as Sleeping Ute Mountain). Standing up here, we're eye to eye with birds in flight. But with flat light, how do I capture any of that? Meanwhile, looking down, I find my leg bleeding, with an astonishing collection of cacti on my calf ("It's only a flesh wound!"). We contemplate cool diagrams from the Park Service and hear good stories from Steve and Porter.

Real versus Ideal
Later the light changes, and I find my groove. Some landscape photographs with dramatic clouds, changing weather, and frame-filling mesas. But do these individual photos tell the whole story? Even if they don't lie, the carefully framed excerpts of time and space paint an idealized picture. The light is striking, but those pink and purple-gray skies and rainbows gave way to heavy winds and a fearsome thunderstorm with tornadoes, rare in the region.

The next day our road led to Butler Wash in Utah, a beautiful, sun-drenched, and sweeping confluence of blue skies and yellow-orange rocks dotted with scrubby green bushes and piñon pines. Tourists, much like us, stop off and hike in to see the "ruins" of a seven-hundred-year-old cliff dwelling across the folded stone canyon. It's difficult to get a picture that takes it all in. Or really see the details. Especially if you stay behind the fence constructed for the safety of both you and the "ruins." From the

Steve Bardolph's shot of interpretive sign and Butler Wash behind.

fence you can't quite sense the sweep of the landscape or get a true idea of the space, the grandeur, or the context. From the overlook, focused on the dwellings, you may forget to look behind at the forested umber hills stretching to the horizon; you might miss the lichen tracing mythical maps and forming fanciful constellations in the sandstone beneath your feet. Any photographs you take won't quite capture the one-hundred-degree heat.

Typical landscape photos, partly due to physics, the lens, and the nature of light, adopt a Renaissance perspective, flattening three-dimensional space into an ideal cropped window, much like a painting with one-point perspective. They can also adopt a "magisterial gaze" and can imply the ethos of "Manifest Destiny," the conquering journey West, especially when taken from designated scenic overlooks. They can obscure, ignore, or warp parts of reality. Traditional photos can make the landscape (or cliff dwellings within it) into something of a commodity.

SPINNING

So what's a photographer to do? How can one possibly capture the feel of a place like Butler Wash? As Porter said, and as Melinda also quotes in her chapter, "Just something as simple as that fence and sign, they alter

Steve Bardolph discusses his Butler Wash panorama. Photograph by Alicia Taylor.

your relationship in the landscape; you get an artificial view. In order to even start to understand this place, you have to go sit over there, or over here, and look at the moving clouds."

This is what I attempt to do in my photographic mosaics. I look around. I scout, sit, stand, wander, and eventually find a spot. A little spot. I take out my camera and zoom in. I get centered, and that often means making sure I'm balanced and grounded enough so I won't fall off a cliff. I start at the horizon and take pictures, left to right, or clockwise, in a spinning motion. One after another, with a little overlap, slowly and patiently clicking frame after frame as I pivot my feet a degree or two at a time. I may take twenty, thirty, or forty photos before I get back to my point of origin and complete a row. Then I point the camera up or down a smidge and start again, frame after frame to document another row as the minutes and clouds begin to flow. Row stacks on row, one, two, three, four, five, six, seven, or in the case of Butler Wash all the way to fifteen, up to the sun and down to my feet as I try to capture everything in my field of view. It's a long and meditative process, and, yes, it can be dizzying. All the while I have no idea what the results will look like, or if they will work at all.

Once back in my studio, these consecutive frames and stacked rows are assembled in a process that may take weeks to form the lavishly detailed 360-degree panoramas I then print as big as I possibly can. In the case of Butler Wash, I spun in place for more than an hour, took more than six hundred photos, and later organized them into a shimmering overall perspective that when printed at five feet high and twenty feet wide gives viewers plenty of satisfying detail to discover. They give some sense of the place as well as the scale of the landscape. The panorama includes details like the hand- and footholds the Ancient Pueblo people used to climb the cliff walls, the counterclockwise path spiraling into the community, various storage and dwelling spaces, and the various members of our team exploring the area. If you look closely, you can find Porter and Steve W. walking up into the hills, David contemplating within a natural stone portal, other tourists watching David from the designated overlook, changing light and even weather, including a rain shower moving in and, with the passage of time in the frames, melting away over the horizon.

COLLABORATION

I'm one of two on the team who bring literal *lenses* to the collaboration. Multiple lenses, and so many frames of view, hundreds within my panoramas, but ironically I'm standing in place, spinning in circles. Is that one perspective or many? What's my point of view?

What is this group doing to shape and reframe my point of view? I sense echoes of my experience as a canoe guide, living for more than a year in a close-knit community on islands within the Boundary Waters Canoe Area Wilderness. I feel the excitement and have the mind-shifting discoveries I had teaching and living for a year in Hungary. We have real human interaction, shared experience and struggle. Since we're in the field together, in the sleet, snow, cold, rain, and uncertainty together, we have a common bond. It's a striking counterpoint to the bland, increasingly corporate infusion/depression of academia. Collaborating with this group picks up a lost childhood thread that traces back to building forts, riding bikes, playing in leaves, and making things, rather than committee meetings, expense reports, syllabi, and academic posturing. We're building and cementing relationships, trust, sharing, camaraderie, and friendship. Then, if we have some important, difficult, challenging circumstance in the future, we can face it together with a solid foundation of trust, respect, and humility.

ASTROFALFA

Joking in the car after a long and exhausting day, gazing at circles of impossibly green center-pivot irrigated fields amid otherwise barren desert, we invent and begin to market astrofalfa. A bright-green plastic panacea for all the problems we face, an enduring corporate answer to the world's increasing woes. I begin to design the T-shirt and logo in my mind, concentric circles, like Target, but on a lime-green ground. No, not circles, but spirals, concentric spirals, left-hand spirals symbolizing the end, the end of all this environmental fretting. Or maybe clockwise and counter-clockwise spirals flowing into each other in an infinite loop.

Team T-shirts: spiraling logo on front with the slogan, "We are field." On the back, "How field are you? TEAM ASTROFALFA." The *A* in Equipo de A has new significance.

We are falfastic. Falfatastic. Falfafastic? "As green as you like it." Roll or spray on. Astrofalfa—available for your fields, lawn, roof, driveway, carpet, and as your foodstuff. Astrofalfa sprouts. Astrosprouts.

"Astrofalfa: it's always green." Or "It's always greener on our side of the fence." We can sponsor a NASCAR car: fluorescent green over a dark-green base that glows in the dark. We'll put a Mobius strip of concentric spirals on the hood and harvest astrofalfa to produce petroleum fuel. We'll use the petroleum fuel to manufacture more astrofalfa. It's an infinite cycle; we've finally closed the loop: perpetual motion and limitless energy.

Celebrate with Falfaschlag Liqueur. Bits of green astrofalfa float like flakes of gold within the bottle. Perfect for St. Patrick's Day, or any day. "Stay thirsty, my friends, but beware, it may give you falfarrhea."

Why do I love this group? In an otherwise serious and profound presentation on the history and culture of the Tewa-speaking Santa Clara Pueblo at Crow Canyon during our first trip together, Porter, on a dare from David, gently inserted the phrase "fields of astrofalfa" into his narrative. Nobody in the audience blinked an eye, and Porter continued his story without even smirking, while Steve W., David, and I, serious academics that we are, giggled into our fists like junior high kids in the back row.

But that alone is not why I love this group. I love that we can joke freely together, but just as easily discuss serious issues of sustainability. We can rant about the shortcomings of academia, and in the next breath whisper our secret hopes and dreams for higher learning with tears in our eyes.

RESPECT AND RESET

Porter spun my head around and changed my perspective when he finished the same presentation noted above with general admonitions for being a better human, gathered from his tribe and elders. How do we relate, teach, ask, and explore, especially when we're from different cultures with different histories, values, customs, and societal norms?

1. Be respectful.
2. Be caring.
3. Be humble.
If you do all this, you'll be good.

Porter also spoke of how the Santa Clara Pueblo is always in search of three things:

1. Beauty: aesthetics and function
2. Harmony: to combat the disharmony
3. Balance: that middle place, a relationship with all things that have life, including trees, clouds, and bears

I've thought about this regularly ever since, and it has affected my photography, design, teaching, relationships, and worldview. Why do we keep quoting Porter? He's about a hundred paces ahead of us on this path, living and breathing respect, caring, humility, beauty, harmony, and balance with every move and word and doing so with a quiet, gentle sense of humor. We're running to catch up, but are distracted by our busy lives in academia and consumer culture.

Why did the Ancient Pueblo people leave the Mesa Verde region? It's one big question for our project, similar for both archaeologists and the National Park Service, worthy of grants and funding. But as Porter answered, simply: maybe it was just time to go. A reset. A time to return to ancient traditions, to restore balance. Our Mesa Verde group instinct seems to be telling us it's nearly time to "go" as well. From our portals in academia amid the din of American materialism and progress, from our travels, time, and discussions together, we're thinking perhaps we (as a research group? as a larger academic community? as a nation? as a species?) need a reset as well.

Back in my undergraduate days, my roommate and I saw the Godfrey Reggio film *Koyaanisqatsi*, a Hopi word for "life out of balance." The film articulated an imbalance I had felt for years but couldn't adequately describe, through the juxtaposition of Philip Glass's insistent, repetitive music and Ron Fricke's time-lapse and slow-motion cinematography of urban life and natural landscapes. I left the film and found a pond where I could cry while I watched the blurry stars reflected in its rippling surface late into the night. My roommate retreated into a blanket cave and didn't speak for three days.

I have enormous respect for Pueblo culture, both ancient and modern, that has the courage, maturity, and tenacity to collectively reset to find better balance. What will it take for me and for our larger society to humble ourselves and face difficult change for the long-term benefit of all species? Do we have it in us? I feel the work our group and many other interdisciplinary communities are doing moves us in the right direction. We're sharing stories and perspectives to foster respect and understanding. We're building connections and relationships to face, with fresh vision and insights, the difficult struggles ahead.

In this Mesa Verde group and in our stories, I sense we're just getting started. We're tapping into something deeper, but we're not there yet. Hints of a larger vision sparkle in our dreams of Astrofalfa University, an (as yet mythical) academic community in Dolores, Colorado, enraptured by the infinite spiral of teaching and learning, with a beautiful flow between art and science and a curious combination of play and serious study. AU, a place to indulge curiosity and adventure, while caring for each other and the earth. Something meaningful, connected, human, and vulnerable, like the mountaintop experiences I've had teaching in Hungary, camping and guiding in the Boundary Waters, biking across Australia, or entering the field with Equipo de A that provide hope, perspective, and optimism.

RIPPLES

Lest we get overly mired in syrupy dreams, I'll conclude my looping verbal mosaic with a few fragments that help to explain the effects of this interdisciplinary collaboration on my research and teaching.

Our group returns again and again to themes of circles, barriers, and boundaries. The Tewa symbol for place, like a target in the sand, like David's ripples in the pond, resonates with the perspective in my sweeping, wide mosaics, with the alternative 360-degree layered circular panoramas I also make, and these in turn provide an interesting and overlapping view of our group's multi-, inter-, and transdisciplinarity.

UMD used to have a thriving Visualization and Digital Imaging Lab, well funded and with a similar mission to that of the UNT Center

Steve Bardolph—360 of Spruce Tree House.

for the Study of Interdisciplinarity, but it's fading into obscurity from lack of participation by overly busy faculty researchers. Thankfully, our entire university is taking up the thread, with a strategic plan that includes interdisciplinarity, cooperation, collaboration, sustainability, and community involvement. Grants and funds will, we hope, hasten this change in orientation. UMD is perhaps stepping into the same waters that ripple between the interactions and research of the Mesa Verde Project.

Steve Wolverton writes about "return on investment" and the skepticism around supporting a research project without clearly defined goals and outcomes. It was a risk for me, too, to embrace this project with such an uncertain endgame while I finished up the last two years of my UMD probationary tenure-track research. I had been scolded for concentrating too much on teaching and service without gaining enough of a national reputation for research. Ironically, despite the gamble and long odds, these Mesa Verde Stories run the home stretch of my research agenda, celebrated by our dean of fine arts as a model for future research within our college of music, theater, art, and design. In large part thanks to the help and collaboration of Equipo de A, I was awarded promotion and tenure.

Kiva Panorama?

This chapter would be incomplete if I didn't admit some of my ignorance and folly, which led to learning and a change in research perspective. Early on, while I was still reading archaeology books in northern Minnesota, I was intrigued by the idea of a panorama from within an open kiva, a perspective from within the bowl of earth beneath a basket of sky. I thought it would be a perfect place to capture the resonance between an Ancient Pueblo worldview and my own spinning, circular photographic methods and create a link with ancient pottery and weaving. Once in the Mesa Verde region, despite my "increasing sensitivity," this previsualized project lingered. I searched for the right kiva and contemplated how I could get my camera gear and myself in and out without leaving a trace. Drop in and climb out? Borrow a ladder? Use a rope?

I finally found the perfect kiva combined with an interesting skyline at the twelfth-century settlement near the Anasazi Heritage Center. I felt uneasy, but sheepishly asked the center's director if I might drop into the kiva for a few minutes to capture my balanced vision of earth and sky. I was met with wide eyes of shock and horror. I didn't think it prudent to ask my follow-up question: "Do you have a ladder I could borrow?"

I'm nauseous recalling the incident and my ignorance and insensitivity. This is where all the discussions of respect before knowledge hit home. I had a research plan for a captivating panorama, but I was entirely missing the point. Even as a member of this research team, I'm an outsider; I'm on the edge, looking in. I was appropriately denied the experience, and I'm embarrassed I ever asked. Sure, the physical occasion of my capture process may leave no trace, at least from my former perspective, but I get dizzy now even thinking about it. This kiva, any kiva, is a sacred space I don't have the ancestry, experience, or invitation to understand. The whole idea now reeks of exploitation and makes me question my motivations. What's my goal? Do I seek to understand with a humble foundation of respect, or am I using Ancient Pueblo history and artifacts to further my own research agenda and ultimately my own promotion and tenure?

Steve Bardolph, kiva contemplation.

Descending into this kiva was out of the question, but I felt myself teetering over another edge. Were any of my photographs in the Mesa Verde region ethically justified?

I want to immerse myself in the landscape, to slow down, notice the details, spend time in space and place, reflect and meditate both during capture and later during weeks of meticulous assembly. I want to connect with the landscape, feel more a part of, rather than apart from. Drink it in. Stay long enough to watch the change in light, temperature, and weather, though the change of seasons would be even better. I want to look closer, experience more, and share the shining grandeur and beauty of it all, but there's the rub. Is it mine to share? Do I have any place here? Is it my story to tell? The experience and adventure are thrilling, but is there also an element of domination, of capture? I'm taking photographs. Seeking to understand, to know more? Yes. But perhaps, like Porter says, I should start with respect. Should I be photographing at all? Is it my place to make these panoramas? If I do, is it my place to share and publish them? I leave no trace when I photograph, but my behavior has consequences. My panoramas may inspire others, even kindle respect and humility, but it's also stoking my ego and reputation through appropriation. And it may inspire more traffic and use of the space, and others may take it further, beyond the fence (is the fence itself respectful or a sign of appropriation?) and into the kiva. I enjoy the process, but there are layers of guilt in the glory. This too may be academic gamesmanship.

I'm still struggling with these questions, but instinct tells me that interdisciplinary sharing of the sort we're engaged in, while entering the field together, may be a solution to this dilemma. Why? No single person or field gets to own the story. Within our team we have an archaeologist, a filmmaker, and a photographer trying to document and make sense of what we find, but we also have a poet, an environmental justice philosopher, and a Native Pueblo person on the team, and each perspective is on the table from the beginning, by design, so we all might question, challenge, inform, and enlighten each other through the process. We're still likely to make mistakes, but there's a greater chance of balanced storytelling when we viscerally share the experience in the field rather than only intellectually at a symposium afterward.

Astrofalfa University in Duluth

After a few trips with Equipo de A, I'm more willing to be vulnerable in my teaching, to ask difficult questions, and to meander through risk and uncertainty while patiently waiting for a spark that may or may not lead to concrete results. Last year, I taught what may be my final crack at the MFA Graduate Seminar and Studio, since we're closing our doors and suspending the program until we have more support and funding. I have years of graduate teaching experience and was ready to introduce my students, like I had before, to the living legends and contemporary themes of graphic design. I painstakingly prepared the semester's syllabus, mapped out projects and readings that would carry us step by methodical step through January, February, March, April, and May. But a week before class started, I realized an opportunity to take my graduate students on a field trip to the Walker Art Center in Minneapolis for *Graphic Design: Now in Production*. Exhibitions of design on this scale come around only once every ten to twenty years, and it would be a shame to miss it.

I drove my graduate students down for a daylong field trip on our first day of class. Together we devoured the show; thrilling were the examples of typography, branding, motion graphics, print, Web, installation, and product design. We experienced, in person, the work of living legends and discussed at length contemporary issues in graphic design. We essentially accomplished in a day everything I had planned for the entire semester. Now what?

We abandoned the syllabus. Shelved our textbooks. Looked to You-Tube, Vimeo, Twitter, and current events for inspiration. After hearing about my research with the Mesa Verde team and learning about the current efforts of AIGA (the professional association for design), my graduate students and I wanted to design for good, to be better humans, to humbly engage our community. We wanted to find a cause, consult experts, and help in whatever way we could with design. This was risky. It took more than a month to agree on a direction. We meandered and bounced between ideas and had more than a few false starts before finally resolving to promote Lake Superior herring as a local, sustainable (and tasty!) food source.

Oddly enough, once we embraced this project of promoting careful harvest of a rebounding fish population right outside our own doors, we had the support and cooperation of local fishermen, chefs, restaurateurs, grocers, and Minnesota Sea Grant. We were an impromptu group of educators, students, scientists, and community members working as equals. We applied for and received a grant. We told a hopeful and inspiring fish story, a glimmer of optimism in the face of the possibility of world oceans being fished out within our lifetimes. We made posters, stickers, and videos. Instead of sitting in a classroom, we rode along in a fishing yawl at sunrise to fetch herring from nets. We gutted, filleted, filmed, cooked, and ate tasty Lake Superior herring. We were invited to speak and present our work at a statewide cook-off and celebration of sustainable fisheries. We cooked herring in the television studio for our local morning news. Amid a rambling process with an uncertain outcome, we shook off cynicism and took risks, followed our curiosity, trusted each other, and had a blast, and it paid off nicely with ripples of collaboration and goodwill across our university, community, and state.

Graphic design is by nature interdisciplinary and collaborative, but my teaching of design hasn't been so in the past. With these recent experiences, I've had a change in attitude. I have more respect for my students and their unique perspectives, their unexplored backstories. I have more training and experience in design than my students, but I'm no longer the lone expert up front. I'm more willing to gently ask and patiently listen while learning collaboratively. We approach the material together with excitement and curiosity, but I do so with a little more humility and uncertainty, willing to question norms, design traditions, and my own assumptions.

My research and photography have likewise changed. I still enjoy seeking new perspectives and engaging with beautiful landscapes, but I'm not a solo genius engaged in a purely aesthetic exercise. Anything I do, as artist, photographer, designer, educator, or scholar, has implications and repercussions. I can't pretend to be designing, teaching, or creating pure form in a vacuum. My work is richer and better informed when I'm out there with others, when we explore, interact, and create together. On a team, whether it's studying in the field or confronting the complex, tangled, and (as the field of graphic design labels them) "wicked problems" we face in society today, results are bound to be more thoughtful, balanced, and positive when we're working together. I'm learning to share and ask for help. My research is part of a larger dialogue and as such has more meaning.

Is there a place for inductive, irreverent interdisciplinarity in academia and society at large? With the proper dose of respect, caring, humility, and humor, we say yes. Is it messy? You bet. Necessary? Absolutely.

The word *spinning* is often used as a term for being out of control or not going forward. "You're spinning off course" or "Stop spinning your wheels." Spinning, however, can also be a way of taking in more than just one viewpoint, a kind of centripetal force, a way of centering. In my panoramas I'm spinning, but really it's no different from the way we struggle with how we imagine our academic place and purpose, no different from the way the world around me is spinning. Knowing if you're off course or centering is always a bit dicey at the beginning. However, when I sit down to the work of final assembly, placing hundreds or thousands of images next to each other to usher in a single panorama, it's not just me that is choosing the individual shots and placement; it's the humor, good cheer, patience, wisdom, and hard work of this group that guide the mouse moving image next to image, the whole of it slowly coming into being.

To view and explore my full-resolution panoramas, visit the following: http://www.stevebardolph.com or these links for each GigaPan individually:

Imagine Living Here—Butler Wash Panorama
http://goo.gl/sMnog5 or http://v.gd/butlerwash
Imagine Living Here—Spruce Tree House Panorama
http://goo.gl/pCRkfA or http://v.gd/sprucetreehouse

The panoramas are also available to view on the *Sushi in Cortez* book page at the University of Utah Press website, www.UofUpress.com.

3

Two Trips to a Brewpub
Stories toward Interdisciplinary Thinking

David Taylor

FIRST TRIP

Dolores River Brewery
Dolores, Colorado
July 25, 2011

> If the universities sponsored an authentic conversation among the
> disciplines, then, for example, the colleges of agriculture would
> long ago have been brought under questioning by the college
> of arts and sciences or of medicine. A vital, functioning intellec-
> tual community could not sponsor patterns of land use that are
> increasingly toxic, violent, and destructive of rural communities.

> —Wendell Berry, *Life Is a Miracle: An Essay against Modern Superstition*

We're having a few pints at the Dolores River Brewery this evening. It
takes a full forty-five minutes for the handmade pizzas to be brought out—
they'll tell you up front that if you don't want to wait, go somewhere else.
Besides, it's a great way to ensure folks getting a pizza will also get another
pint while waiting. I'm having an IPA, one of the best I've ever tasted, but
I think the strong flavors (piney florals, I offer) are as much the company
as the brew—both are outstanding.

Steve Wolverton (archaeologist), Steve Bardolph (photographer), and
Porter Swentzell (Tewa Pueblo consultant) have been my companions for
the day—we've been visiting and exploring Ancient Pueblo sites—Sand
Canyon, Edge of the Cedars, Butler Wash, and Hovenweep. We've driven
a two-hundred-mile loop from Cortez, Colorado, to Monticello, Utah,

Imagine Living Here—Butler Wash Panorama. Photo mosaic by Steve Bardolf.

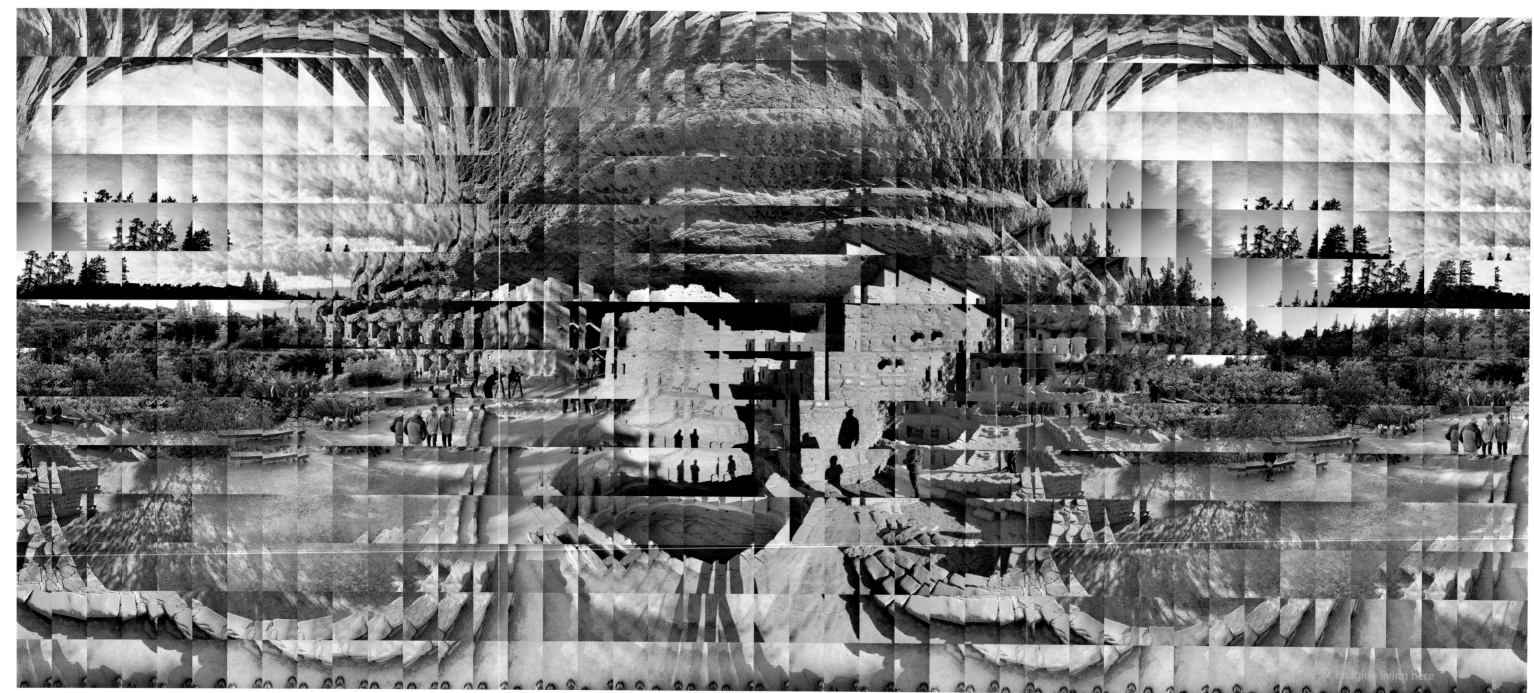

Imagine Living Here—Spruce Tree House Panorama. Photo mosaic by Steve Bardolf.

David Taylor writes in his journal at Sand Canyon.

through Blanding to Hovenweep National Monument and back to Crow
Canyon Archaeological Center, our home for the week. Of course, at
the end of the long day of driving and talk, we sidestepped dinner at the
Crow Canyon cafeteria for a beer and pizza here.

The conversation varied widely during the day—from discussions
about art and archaeology to Mesa Verde sites and Pueblo culture. Perhaps best, though, was the good humor shared, which made being in the
van with others for six hours pleasant. The topics alternated between serious (Porter offering his thoughts on the lines between science and heritage,
Steve W. rethinking the role of science, and Steve B. and I offering what
the art of words and visuals can and can't offer) and silly. The highlight of
the talk came as we were heading toward Hovenweep through iconic arid
southwestern landscape.

In the middle of all this brown and red was a pasture of alfalfa so
green and vibrant that it seemed as though someone had taken their stick
of green out of their sixty-four box of Crayolas and filled in this square.
All of us were struck by its Monty Pythonesque "Now, for something completely different." We all knew that the real reason for such an unreal sight
was the use and abuse of water in a landscape where a lush green is *not*
a natural phenomenon. It was Porter who offered the term to accurately
describe our thoughts on the too green field. He said, "Yes, it's astrofalfa."

The conceit of the joke extended throughout the rest of the day. We
talked of "astrofalfa" products (everything from a cure for the common cold
to the answer for renewable energy) and the commercials we'd create to
market them. We coined words such as *astrorific* and *falfatastic* to use in our
marketing and thoughts about how to use social media to never have to pay
an ad agency. We talked about how we'd use our astrofalfa billions to fund
our idylls. In other words, the rest of the drive passed in a lot of silliness
between four grown men traveling in a van to Ancient Pueblo sites for the
serious work of reimagining the history and engagement of these places.

Northeast across the intersection at the Dolores River Brewery was
an abandoned three-story building that must have been a grand ski lodge
in its past—eight gabled windows on one side and three in the front, an
oddly inviting door situated on the corner of the building. It is an impos-
ing structure for the tiny downtown, the kind of place that you know at
some point someone put a lot of money into, in belief of her dreams.

One of us pointed out the window to the building and offered, "Here's
where we can open Astrofalfa University, a university that transcends all the

David Taylor imagines the first building of Astrofalfa University in Dolores.

divisions and failings of the modern university." After about five minutes of laughter, we each began to point to which window would be our office, the classes we'd offer, the administration that would allow us to create any class our imagination could come up with, and the freedom we'd have to converse with other faculty beyond any notion of disciplinary boundary.

It would be easy to dismiss this conversation as another silly extension of "astrofalfa" talk fueled by good brew, but something from that has stayed with me long after the beer and laughter sobered up. That is a core belief in the innovative possibilities of transdisciplinary and interdisciplinary work, the need for collegiality and personal humility among faculty, the acceptance of appropriate boundaries, and, as Wendell Berry puts it, membership in "the fate of affected communities"—meaning we are responsible for not just our teaching and scholarship but our broader communities too.

Dreams and the UNT EESAT Building

Steve W. and I have the good fortune of having offices at the University of North Texas's Environmental Education, Science, and Technology Building, or EESAT as we call it. It was completed in 1998 and was dedicated to the idea that environmental scientists in all their disparate fields should share working space with other faculty in the humanities in order to create unique and innovative ways of engaging and tackling questions of outreach, community involvement, ethical choice, and commitment to sustainability. During a typical day, our building is filled with university students attending classes in geology, geography, philosophy, entomology, hydrology, archaeology, toxicology, and, when I can offer one, an environmental writing class. EESAT also houses the Elm Fork Education Center, an environmental education center for K–fifth graders in the area. Thus, our lobby may be the most diverse grouping of people you'll find on an American university campus.

In the lobby, a plaque dedicating the building reminds us, "Environmental education is putting the sciences and arts together for the purpose of understanding our environment" (Aldo Leopold, "The Role of Wildlife in a Liberal Education"). When those of us who work in the EESAT are at our best, this is our motto.

It's a belief I've long held—from my undergraduate and master's studies through my PhD and beyond. As an undergraduate in English, I spent many of my weekends hiking and backpacking through any local woods I could find. My summers were spent at a camp not far from Denton; as a counselor and recreation director, I learned how to make sumac "lemonade" and horsemint tea, when to pick blackberries and mulberries at their ripest, how to get to the wild plums before the birds do. I taught folks how to tell poison ivy from box elder and how to make a tasty salad from a field. All the while, I had my poetry books, and whether it was Wordsworth or Gary Snyder, I knew the words on the page had an intimate, old connection to this other knowledge and learning of place.

As a master's student, I had the good luck of meeting Max Oelschlaeger, one of environmental philosophy's founding figures. Of course, our connection came about by my venturing over to the philosophy department because I couldn't find professors in English who could guide me in my link between landscape and literature. Max taught me to go beyond any idea of departments and to reimagine my reading not so much as poetry, fiction, philosophy, policy, and so on, but as expressions of a cellular drive in us to understand and connect with nature and ourselves, or, in his terms, *wildness*.

When I started my PhD, I had the good fortune of studying with George Hutchinson, an American studies scholar who happened to be in an English department. Thus, during my dissertation research, on Saturday mornings when we would row the two-person scull down the Tennessee River, George directed me to read not just the literary community's view of Thoreau, but to read broadly about Thoreau's interest in the science of his time. This approach to looking at early American natural history as a way into place gave me the idea for my first book when I moved to South Carolina for a faculty job. For the next three summers, I traveled to Caroliniana Library at the University of South Carolina for archival research and to the field to see what remained of the landscape described by those naturalists between 1700 and 1860.

The best way to put it is that I've never had a typical academic education—whether that is of my own curmudgeonly eccentricities or the good luck of meeting some outstanding mentors who saw beyond the limits of their fields, I don't know. Over and over, I was told by my mentors, "Do work that draws from all your interests and skills. It *is* all connected." Too, they reminded me to walk over to other departments and ask questions when you are studying outside your expertise. This is learning, they said. This passionate curiosity is partly what one should mentor, so never lose it! Only then may you "understand your environment," as Aldo Leopold would say.

When designing the EESAT Building, some brilliant person realized that the way to make sure such disparate faculty would interact is to place the bathrooms on the far side from our offices. We all must traverse a wide walkway from our caves/offices. We nod as we pass each other, sometimes we say hello, and sometimes we even begin to talk about our various projects and work.

This is how some of the best projects I have been involved with have happened. One of us slows to say hello, the other squeezes his or her legs to listen and talk, and then says, "I'll be right back. Let's sit and talk." I've had creative writing students work with graduate students in environmental science while paddling forty miles of the Brazos River, reenacting part of John Graves's trip fifty years ago that led to his book *Goodbye to a River*. We've created an annual event titled "eARTh day: a celebration of environmental arts, music, writing, and film," which offers students the chance to present their art in our building. This is the way Steve W. and I started a conversation that has led to this project, this moment. What do an environmental scientist/archaeologist and a poet have in common? What we found in common was a belief that education is more than a classroom full of rote PowerPoints and that our jobs represent more than hoarding majors to our departments. It should be a creative journey for students and faculty as well. We found that each of us had read widely and taken on projects that pushed the definitions of our discipline. We also found at the heart of our conversation an understanding that as we began to tell our stories of our fields, we also had a common story of commitment to thoughtful choices about our environment.

From our discussion, Steve W. and I organized a panel discussion with other faculty who've taken their scholarship into social and environmental issues. Two UNT faculty members, Melinda Levin, a documentary film-maker, and Rob Figueroa, a philosopher interested in environmental justice, joined our group. The panel presentation taught us that to this point all we've done is talk about our separate work. Now we needed a singular project for us to take on.

Steve W. suggested we head west and look into the Ancient Pueblo sites of the Southwest. He'd done research there for years but also knew the entire story hadn't been told. Thus, with a generous grant from UNT's Center for the Study of Interdisciplinarity, we headed west.

Collegiality and Humility
  From Denton, Texas, to Santa Fe, New Mexico
  July 23, 2011

> Give me for my friends and neighbors wild men, not tame ones. The wildness of the savage is but a faint symbol of the awful ferity with which good men and lovers meet.
> —Thoreau, "Walking"

Steve W. and I started the drive to Sante Fe and our campground at eight. We talked of families, children, backgrounds, and histories, personal and not. The West Texas towns clicked by one by one in good and pleasant conversation, Vernon, Quanah, Childress, Memphis, Clarendon, Claude, and then Amarillo. It wasn't substantive talk for two people who make their livings in a university, but it was important because we shared what mattered to us and why we've come to believe these things matter so much. In other words, we were offering each other what we "savagely" love in our lives and so that when we began to take on "substantive" topics like interdisciplinarity, we knew something of the feral terrain of the other's life. Outside of Amarillo, we smiled as the Southwest began as we left the wide flatness of West Texas and descended into a canyon where the first cholla cacti appeared beside the road, the mesas rose on the western horizon, and monsoon rains swelled in the sky above them.

Story is the word we've been tossing about this project. The *Oxford English Dictionary* (*OED*) offers this etymology: Anglo-Norman *estorie* (Old French *estoire*, later in semilearned form *histoire*) < Latin *historia*. One aspect of our use of *story* is our interest in the *history* of the Mesa Verde people and their story. This story will be offered to us in ruins, in restored sites, in the potsherds in the sand, in the interpretive brochures, in the Pueblo stories Porter chooses to share, in the broad culture and simulacra decades of tourism have brought to the area, and, of course, in the archaeology. Another aspect is the *story* each of us will tell from our discipline—in other words, our story. I knew I'd be looking for the "poetry" of things—the place, the art and artifact, the idiosyncrasies and awkward archetypes, the meme of a T-shirt with the Cliff Palace on it, the moment I shiver when tracing my finger over a thumbprint on a piece of eight-hundred-year-old pottery—and I would, with offerings to Calliope, Vishnu, kachinas, Isaiah, Thoreau, Robinson Jeffers, and other muses, write poetry.

Among the many definitions the *OED* offers for story is "An incident, real or fictitious, related in conversation or in written discourse in order to amuse or interest, or to illustrate some remark made." This sense of story is what we're using—the story that's created in good conversation and in having to listen and ask questions to learn. This sense of story is one where you offer a thought or a photograph and realize it will be reimagined by someone else in the group because she isn't from your field and doesn't have the same background. Here would be a good place to launch into a discussion of hermeneutics, but suffice it to say that this broader definition is to elucidate "some remark made," and the remark being made is not one voice but six disparately speaking in one story. However, for this reimagination and questioning to take place, there has to be trust, goodwill, and people of "awful ferity." All my mentors and my closest friends live this way—with good wildness and wild goodness.

As Steve W. and I parked the car at the Rancheros de Sante Fe Campground, ate some snacks, opened a beer, and ambled into the piñon-juniper forest to smoke good cigars, I realized we'd taken one of the first steps, creating something more than collegiality, trust enough to ask about what we don't know and trust enough to listen well.

I am still in the dark,

except for the stamp of a dry moon in the peach and turquoise
morning sky

and the jagged imprint and resting Sandia Mountains to
the west.

Here, in July, on this dawn, the monsoon flowers open
themselves to light,

while the scent of piñon pitch bends itself around me

like a bracelet of water.

I am still dreaming of afternoon rains, not sure if I am awake,

making a way into the shape and buzz of sandstone, heat
clouds, and rising colors.

Santa Fe, New Mexico
  July 24, 2011

Our route from Santa Fe to Farmington would be through a ten-thousand-
foot pass in the San Juans, cool air and green, wet fields of flowers, over to
Chama, and then into the drier, warmer clime of Farmington. Along the
way, we made our first stop at an Ancestral Puebloan site, Aztec Ruins, a
national park in Aztec, New Mexico. The site is well organized, and the
self-guided tour allows visitors to roam relatively freely among the ruins.
There is something a little odd about visiting Aztec Ruins—a little like
you've stumbled into a backwater national park, the kind of place they
send the newbie rangers or interns without connections. The museum in
the visitors' center has the feel of an exhibit in need of an update—just
too much dust on the diorama. The walls and doors of West Ruin have
been rebuilt enough to allow one to walk through a maze of corridors.
Steve showed me the ancient mortar lines versus the restored work. We
walked the courtyard and descended into the heavily restored and rebuilt
Great Kiva. Earl Morris, a young archaeologist, was in charge of excavat-
ing, stabilizing, and rebuilding the Great Kiva (completed in 1934). It is
impressive to descend the stairs into a partially submerged, covered round
room. The temp drops some fifteen to twenty degrees, and sunlight comes
in only from the hole in the ceiling and the entrance and exit—though
there is ambient artificial light. A ubiquitous soundtrack of drumming
and chanting fills the space, and as my eyes adjusted I could see the neatly

adobe-smoothed walls in colors that I was assured were the same as those Morris saw in the ruins. There is some debate about the height of the ceiling, currently at about eight feet above ground level; most archaeologists would say it is four to six feet too high. Off to one side, two boys practiced their balance walking along the raised-foot drum rectangles as their mother watched for rangers. Steve W. and I shrugged our shoulders and exited, and as we entered the light, we asked each other about the experience. "I guess I wonder what's authentic," I said. "That's a hard question," Steve W. answered with an impish smile.

Steve W. talked about the difficulty archaeologists and the Park Service face. "How do you engage visitors in a site while preserving it to allow for future research?" A preserved site can mean one that looks like a pile of rubble to the average visitor, but is intact and full of research possibilities to the archaeologist. Also, what is respectful to the dignity of the site and those who are members of descendant cultures? Leave it totally untouched? Restore it to increase tourism? Somewhere in between?

We needed to pick up Steve W.'s old friend from Minnesota Steve Bardolph, our photographer on the trip, at the Farmington Airport. It is a nice, clean, small airport—we were handed Steve B.'s checked bags through an open bay door to the tarmac. Steve B. laughed that this could be a weak link in Homeland Security; we agree al-Qaeda must never find out about Farmington. The drive to Cortez gave the two Steves a chance to catch up with each other—they've been friends since kindergarten. There was a lot of lowdown on living in Duluth and Brainerd and surviving a winter in the Boundary Waters, the accuracy and stereotypes of the Cohen brothers' *Fargo*, and, of course, what the heck we were trying to pull together in this project—still in the process of definition, Steve W. explained. When we arrived at Crow Canyon Archaeological Center, we met up with Porter Swentzell, our Tewa consultant. Porter would provide us a Puebloan cultural context to our project, but more so, as I found, he'd also provide a lot of thoughtful and comedic insight.

Immediately after our introductions, we were invited to join a group of interns traveling to a local site, Yucca House. Yucca House is a national monument site and is thus protected, but it is also remote, and no road signs point to its location among private farms. As a park brochure states:

> Today, Yucca House is surrounded by productive agricultural lands and has beautiful views across the Montezuma Valley.

Although many archeological sites in the region have disappeared through urban development or have been irreparably damaged by vandalism, Yucca House National Monument will remain protected well into the future. The long-term preservation of Yucca House ensures that archeologists will be able to continue studying Ancestral Puebloan society and what caused them to migrate from this region in the late 1200s.

When we arrived at Yucca House, we ascended a mound of rocks and dirt with an empty center; near and far I could see circular mounds of the same. It was a beautiful view, with Mesa Verde in the East and monsoon clouds and rain covering the top. Yucca House is well preserved, we were told—research is ongoing and will be because of its relatively undisturbed condition. Mark Varien, research and education chair at Crow Canyon, offered us details and descriptions, helping to deepen our vision of Yucca House beyond the rubble we were standing on. I wondered, though, if this wasn't part of the project. How would I feel if I had lucked upon a note mentioning Yucca House, followed the map provided on the website, and walked to the top of this rubble mound alone? Would it be more authentic than what I felt leaving the Great Kiva at Aztec Ruins? Will I always need an interpreter/archaeologist to make sense of and see the deeper story in the rubble?

Over Mesa Verde, the monsoon storm was slowly rolling off the western slope and beginning to move toward us. The story Mark told us about Yucca House was so engaging that we lingered as lightning strikes came closer. One finally hit no more than a mile away and broke the trance of Mark's words. We quickly scrambled for the cars and drove home in a driving rain. Later, we heard that a tornado touched down not far from Yucca House, the first in this area in decades. Steve W., Steve B., Porter, and I rolled out our sleeping bags under a porch covering at Crow Canyon because the rain was torrential.

Appropriate Boundaries

A poetics without a concurrent ethnopoetics is stunted, partial, therefore faulty at a time like ours that can only save itself by learning to confront its multiple identities and definitions—its contradictions, therefore, & its problematics.

—Jerome Rothenberg, "Ethnopoetics at the Millennium"

Cortez Journal, July 21, 2011, "Twister Hits Land near Towaoc."

Crow Canyon Archaeological Center
July 25, 2011

I was certainly not the first up, as the sun was already topping the eastern ridge and I could hear coffee-roused voices coming from the direction of the cafeteria. But I slept well between the sound of rain and the sprinklers periodically spitting out gray water over the lawn just off the porch where we were sleeping.

At the bottom of the sloped lawn was a retention pond of brown water, rimmed on the eastern shore by moisture-happy cottonwoods. The western slope had nicely stacked thick slabs of sandstone. I took my sleeping pad down to the pond to sit seiza and count breaths. On the pond were water skimmers and other insects dotting the surface; a kingfisher arced down from side to side, catching minnows. "Circles and circles," I whispered just over a breath.

At breakfast Steve B., Steve W., Porter, and I talked more—and more than about the tornado that touched down near Yucca House last night. Porter detailed his drive in from Santa Clara Pueblo, near Santa Fe. Perhaps best in our conversation was a bit of a fire in each

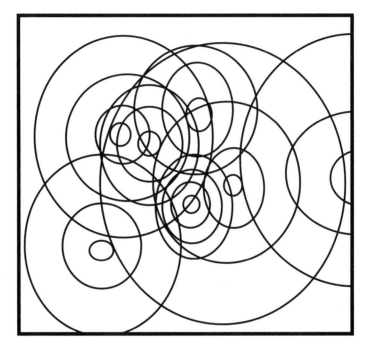

Circles. Illustration by David Taylor.

of us about our work and also a lot of laughter, good humor, and humility.

On the drive to Sand Canyon, the rest of us listened as Porter told us a bit more about his Tewa Pueblo community in Santa Clara. He discussed the matrilineal and patriarchal lines, religious divisions of winter and summer, and within those the lineages and names. He said that only recently have Tewa people begun to take their father's name; before, it was always their mother's name.

I wrote down much of what Porter was saying in my journal, in part as an oral history of his community; I was writing it down in part because I am a writer—I write; I was also writing it down because I was wondering about the questions of ethnopoetics, which have been hounding me throughout the project. I listened carefully to Porter's words, but felt the line of appropriation grow fuzzy.

I amended these notes by asking Porter about definitions and interpretations, but in the end I took down his words, symbols, and ideas. Thus, I was also, in some ways, *taking* them. It was this kindness on Porter's part that made me feel discomfort about what I might be offering in return. What gift could I return? Should this relationship have reciprocal boundaries?

Ethnopoetics has been a part of my reading since 1982, when I happened across Gary Snyder's *The Old Ways*. However, most of my actual work within it was more of a dabbling, as I lifted quotes from one place or another for scholarly or poetic inspiration. For the first time in twenty years of reading, I had to actually engage in the challenges of ethnopoetics. In his essay "The Politics of Ethnopoetics," Snyder writes, "An expansionist imperialist culture feels most comfortable when it is able to believe that the people it is exploiting are somehow less than human. When it begins to get some kind of feedback that these people might be human beings like themselves it becomes increasingly difficult." Perhaps this feeling about boundaries is what Snyder describes, not so much the feeling of sameness and potential assimilation, but the dark, honest bearing witness to meaningful difference and the equally growing sense of respect. Perhaps thoughtful discomfort is the beginning of a relationship across cultures. My friendship with Porter can be the free and easy exchange of jokes, commiseration about classes, administration, and such, but my work with Porter must come from a different exchange. In borrowing from him, I am also taking, and the poetry I offer in return heightens the risk of arrogance, imperialism, and, equally bad, the mistreatment of a friend.

This thought brings me back, though, to my relations with the group. I can always use the terminology of my field to put myself in a position of power within the group—they don't know my field. But to what end? "My comfort," as Snyder might say? Within academics, a scholar should know her field well, but when does that easily slip into the too comfortable judgment of other fields of study, or when do we within our field begin doing harm to our communities (academic, local, and nonhuman)? Maybe ethnopoetics and interdisciplinarity aren't so different in their greater lesson.

We reached the site at Sand Canyon in a half hour. The site is self-touring and not on a main route, so it's pretty quiet here. It's a piñon-juniper forest and looked relatively lush after the previous night's rain. Porter walked through the forest as though he was at a Trader Joe's on free-sample day—late-season wild spinach here, Mormon tea there. He pulled a few piñon needles and handed them to me. "Chew them only on the tip of your tongue," he suggested. It tasted like piney lemon.

We talked about what most scholars say was the reason these folks left their homes and places in this region around the same time (around AD 1285)—drought, food shortage, and warfare. Certainly, the scientific data from the various "——ists" point to these causes. I had no problem with

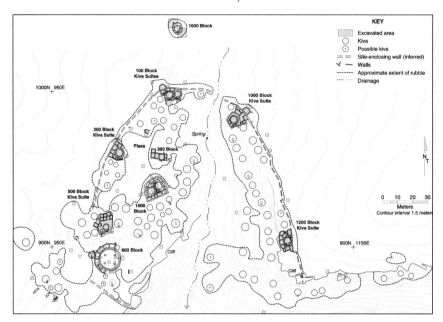

Sand Canyon interpretive map (Courtesy of Crow Canyon Archaeological Center).

the idea—no vested interest in my sense of scholarship, history, or place. Porter might, but it seemed that he was more interested in possibilities than conclusions.

For example, when he looked at the sign, which showed the rooms and structure of the Sand Canyon dwellings, Porter saw lines of division between lineages and clans and families. "Maybe," he said, "they just got tired of living in the same place." Or maybe the drought was for them a reminder to try to remedy their lives, which had deviated from their spiritual goals—to start anew, which also means returning to the old ways. In the sand, he drew this symbol:

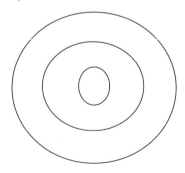

Illustration by David Taylor.

He said this is a Tewa symbol that could be simplified as "place." Community is a type of "place," but not necessarily the only kind of "place." Another synonymous meaning is "center of." He said when these ideas are combined with other images, the actual context comes to life.

I noticed in the symbol circles, which, on one hand, can be seen as smaller and smaller—focusing in. On the other, I saw in it circles growing out just as I saw in the pond this morning—circles growing out that must inevitably intersect with other "centers of." Of course, then, I couldn't help but apply this creative reading to Porter's thoughts about this place, the choices of the people who were here, their loves and fears, their listening to the weather and land as judgment of their choices and renewal of their path. Here the intersection opens; here the intersection leads to loss.

David Taylor and circles at Sand Canyon Pueblo, a symbol for place or community. Photograph by Steve Bardolph.

I was also thinking about whether this was my line of appropriation. Was I seeing in the symbol what I wanted to see, or was I listening? Was I opening myself fully to the "contradictions & its problematics," as Rothenberg would claim? Was I respectful of Porter and what his Tewa Pueblo words, symbols, and thoughts were offering me? Was I just as respectful of Steve W. and what science and my own language had given me?

We talked a lot between us about why for generations tourists have loved these ancient dwellings—Americans, Europeans, and Japanese by the busloads. What are they looking for? It isn't their past, but for the few with an ancestral heritage. They'll ask the silliest questions. Porter said the number-one question folks ask is "Where did they poop?" But the desire for something is sincere and maybe even more so because they can't articulate it.

For me, I was looking for an old and respectful language—older than the etymologies of the *OED* but in love with my blood knowledge of English vowels and consonants. I know that's my linguistic heritage, but I don't want to be bound by it. I wanted a story that's older than the syllables I could produce yet bore with it all the ambiguity of what I just wrote. I wanted my language and story to be that moment when the tourist is at a loss for words and connects with something still and possibly sacred. I wanted a clean sentence as tough as sinew yet aware and pliable. But sitting in the backseat of the van and writing in my journal, I was uncomfortable; this was as it should be. The words and ideas I was noting were in part mine and in part not mine at all. But I was trying with every line to nod to its origin. Maybe even more, I was trying to let the words I wrote down be words that were listening to the stories I was hearing, to be respectful of the boundaries between cultures and disciplines.

Membership

> The only remedy I can see is for scientists (and artists also) to understand and imagine themselves as members of, and sharers in, the fate of affected communities. Our schools now encourage people to regard as mere privileges the power and influence they call leadership. But leadership without membership is a terrible thing.
>
> —Wendell Berry, *Life Is a Miracle: An Essay against Modern Superstition*

My friends and I are still laughing about all that we could accomplish at Astrofalfa U. Some of the thoughts are quips about the silliness of

Community

In the pond,
dragonflies and water skimmers lightly dot the water
as a kingfisher swoops in arc from side to side
catching minnows and perch,

small circles across the water.

The sand,
the circles of the pond,
each break on the water and score in the dirt,
another place, another center,
grows and reaches out,
crosses into others,

sand intersecting the water.

All our places open and cross—
dragonfly, red rock, notebook,
a turning wing, handprint pictographs,
a trail teaching our feet to walk,
the green of a ripe juniper berry,
a dark line of sediment writing where water runs during the monsoon rains—
circles drawn in water and soil,
letting the words written down
be words that are listening.

"Community," a poem by David Taylor.

our respective departments, colleges, and universities; some are serious thoughts masquerading as humor about classrooms, education, creativity, and collegiality. There is something, though, worth teasing out.

The more we expand our conversation about universities, the more we realize the dangers of staying comfortably in our fields and departments. By putting on these blinders, we run the risk of doing harm because those from other fields are not asking us questions that we cannot articulate for ourselves—that is, some penetrating, challenging questions are more than unasked; they are lost. If we believe the university should play a leadership role (meaning more than an influx of cash) in a community, then we have to listen to what our respective disciplines might be ignoring. We have to see that intellectualism isn't just succeeding in peer-reviewed journals in our field (sure, that's part of it), but that the deeper intellectualism is imagining all the possible impacts and applications of our thought and creativity. Too, isn't that what we want for our students? To offer them not just training that will provide them a fair income but an education that offers them ideas on sustainable ways to become citizens and to live as though they are active members of their neighborhood, their community, and their bioregion?

Here's another way of saying this. I want to write poetry, but to write poetry that doesn't have any connection and commitment to my place, my home, my family, my friends, and my communities runs the risk of being, as Berry puts it, "toxic, violent, and destructive." Any field of study that isolates itself runs the risk of doing harm to itself, perhaps to other fields of study, but, most important, to the world beyond the university.

Ken Dickson, a scientist friend, told me a story of when he quit enjoying English classes. A teacher asked the students to write a poem about a flower. He raised his hand and asked, "What species?" She responded, "Oh, it doesn't matter." He said he couldn't shake his thoughts of spring and early-summer bluebonnets, paintbrush, plains coreopsis, black-eyed Susans, pinwheels, and late-summer liatris, Joe-Pye weed, and goldenrod, and so he said he could not write a poem. He said he avoided literature classes from then on. He went on to become an environmental scientist because he needed to understand the details to know how to respond at all to nature. Even then, though, he found that science could not set policy or motivate people to conservation, preservation, action, or caring. It was then he realized he needed to bring folks from other fields together to make any sustainable changes. In the early 1990s, Ken offered up an idea at UNT—why not build a building, bringing together faculty from differing fields who have an interest in the environment? Thus, the EESAT Building was conceived; Ken is its father. The Mesa Verde group is only one of his children.

Putting together a transdiciplinary and interdisciplinary group to develop a response to the sites of Ancient Pueblo culture will in itself do nothing for the ideals in the above paragraph. It might be a glimpse into how such ideals can begin, but in itself it is a small shuffle forward. Behind it, though, is Astrofalfa University; that is the ideal that could drive forward something deeper and more important. In all of its silliness, it is easy to dismiss such talk. We should not, though, dismiss its impetus.

I have another sip of the tart and hoppy India pale ale and stare at the old ski lodge. I'm dreaming of Astrofalfa U and how I could shape classes around ideas, not disciplines; how I could bring in colleagues and friends to fill in the gaps in fields where I am weak; and how I could encourage students to follow their ideas, not academic tradition and discipline. These are the people I want to watch graduate—those with a wildness to their thoughts. I'm also listening to Steve W., Steve B., and Porter laugh and talk in fields ranging from communication design to protein residues in potsherds to how to prune a juniper sapling so that it becomes a single trunk, which makes for a strong bow. I'm wishing Melinda and Rob were here too, because I know they'd broaden the conversation and deepen it too. Someone throws out another "Astrofalfa" joke, and we all come close to the grade school "milk out the nose" moment of laughter.

SECOND TRIP

Dolores River Brewery
Dolores, Colorado
October 6, 2011

Two and a half months later, the whole group came to the area. Rob and Melinda joined the four of us who were here in the summer—Steve W., Steve B., Porter, and me. We tented at the Mesa Verde National Park campground. What began as a pleasant, cool evening turned into a night of driving wind and rain and then to sleet and snow. We bonded in the midtwenty-degree morning around a fire and later huddling over cups of warm coffee in the camp store not far away.

We made some of the same trips the rest of us had this summer—Sand Canyon, Butler Wash—but we decided to skip Hovenweep and Edge of the Cedars to take in Escalante, Goodman Point, and those sites within Mesa Verde National Park, Balcony House, Cliff Palace, and Spruce Tree House. The longest drive from our campground was Butler Wash, so we dedicated the bigger part of this day to that effort. For some reason, the four of us from this summer had felt that was our high point, and we wanted to share this place with Melinda and Rob.

When we arrived we went about our usual ways—Steve B. listening and taking literally thousands of pictures; Porter wandering along the trail, chewing on what's there to be chewed on and asking the closest person nearby to try; and Steve W. offering an archaeologist's point of view only when asked. Usually, I'm wandering off with my journal, but this time I offered Melinda to serve as part-time technical assistant, carrying cameras or equipment to make her filming work easier. I told her secretly that I'd always loved the idea of seeing my name in the credits of a film as "key grip" or "best boy," even though I had no idea what those terms meant.

Rob and Porter wandered off to the opposite side of the canyon head to sit and chat. Steve B. went about his photography ways. On the right side of the ruins a bit off the trail, there's a small arch or natural bridge, and if it was raining a small wash would run through it and pour into the valley below. Inside the arch are handprint pictographs, mostly of the right hand. Porter told us that these generally mean life, and the left means death or an end. We each took our turn looking, photographing, or filming respectfully. I took some time with my journal and didn't write a word, letting the pen hover over the paper, listening to the friends I was with and the land I was in and learning to care more deeply for both.

It was a fascinating time to watch our group work at a site yet not have much to do with each other directly. Steve B. and Melinda needed time to work alone; Rob and Porter talked about things away from the group, and I, having been there during the summer, was hounding Melinda about how to help her. She finally got me out of her hair by asking me to make some footage with the Super8 camera. "Of what?" I asked. "Anything. Just somewhere else," she laughed. Thus, I found the trail to the bottom of the canyon and the dry riverbed below. There's a sparse trail there through the tall grass, reed, cottonwood, and gamble oak. For some reason, I took to running through it with the camera held hip high. Why? I don't know. I guess I wanted to take in the movement of wind and water.

Butler Wash

At the bottom of the canyon,
I'm running through the grass, reeds, and willows
to where the water falls from the cliff above the ruins.
Where the drops spatter,
the sand is washed away
and only rock remains.

Above the dwellings,
in a water-carved bowl in the sandstone
beneath a small arch
are red handprints,
some of the right hand,
one of the left.

When I sit long enough
and let even my journal become quiet,
the wind coming off the mountain
hums down the riverbed
and through the archway,
as though a flute.

Water is the dream of rock,
not merging,
but already singular,
as air imagines itself in summer fire,
waiting on the wooded ridge above,
fire erodes to stone,
air follows the riverbed,
in spirals of entering or leaving,
a fluteplayer of lightning strikes
lifting birds and butterflies to flight.

Perhaps an hour or two later, we somehow came together on the ridge above the ruins. There we each sat and told a bit of our thoughts about the place and speculated about what we might do as a group, the best part being that we didn't really worry too much about the answer. Soon a group of Japanese tourists covered head to toe in long pants and long-sleeved shirts, with large floppy hats to keep the UV rays out, appeared. "Onegai shimasu," and they held the camera out and gathered for a group picture.

The trip back was a more direct route, so we missed the summer's "astrofalfa fields." By then, Rob and Melinda had heard the whole thing over and over. So, too, at the end of the day, we headed to our old haunt from the last time. The six of us sat laughing and talking about our day and its possibilities. A couple of us pointed to the ski lodge and told Rob and Melinda our plan for Astrofalfa U. They understood fully and asked for their offices as well. From a table not far from us, two archaeologists Steve W. knew joined us and asked for their faculty slots as well. Before the evening was through, we had even signed up our first few students from people eavesdropping on our good cheer.

At one point I sauntered to the bar to have a beer separate from the group and the folks who had joined us. The crowd kept growing around the tables we had pulled together, but this was as it should be. As academics, it's hard to remember sometimes that we still long to be a part of and responsible to a group, preferably a group that is inclusive and grows when there are tolerance, humility, and good cheer about it. We each get into our routines, which instead of becoming the softness of ritual often become the rigidity of habits. I guess my act of faith in interdisciplinary work is that after we've had these kinds of experiences—in the field, in conversation, in listening, in laughter, in musing, in posing answerless questions in a pub in Dolores— somewhere down the road they grow into tangible products. A poem that has

David Taylor writing in his journal at Natural Bridge, Butler Wash.

David Taylor and Porter Swentzell look upward under natural bridge, Butler Wash.
Photograph by Rob Figueroa.

so little to do with the poet because it is the group's poem, not his. A film in which each of us has been partly holding the camera. A photograph holding each of our points of view. An archaeology shot through with the myths of the studied culture. A philosophy of fingertips and wind. A Pueblo myth that invites and also asks for privacy in the same words. Were this volume made up of only this narrative, it would be worse for it because the story that needs to be told is the sum of each of the essays. It is a narrative bigger than any one of our voices, and the confusion we've kept expressing to this point is a kind of early wisdom. Maybe in this way, the worst of reason can give way to the best of faith, and the product that comes about might not be so different.

The sharp aftertaste of the IPA on my tongue offers me another metaphor to laugh about as I join my friends and the possibility of more good work and the poetry they offer me, or, I should say, in the community they offer me.

CHAPTER

4

Irrigating Astrofalfa

Porter Swentzell

In May 2011 I received a call from a man who identified himself as somehow being connected with the Crow Canyon Archeological Center. After several minutes of explaining a project that he was working on with other people, he said that he was looking for someone to provide cultural perspective on the Mesa Verde region. Someone at Crow Canyon had recommended me to him. The details of the project appeared vague, but I had experience doing similar kinds of things with Crow Canyon before, and I also had spent time doing cultural interpretation at my tribal park: Puye Cliff Dwellings. When the man on the phone offered some money for my time, it sealed the deal. I said okay with only the most cursory understanding of the project.

In July 2011 I finally met the man on the phone, Steve Wolverton, along with a couple more members of the team: David Taylor (a poet) and Steve Bardolph (a photographer). We gathered at Crow Canyon, where we would spend the next few days camping, visiting sites, chasing mosquitoes, and looking for shade. On the first evening we headed to a site in the valley between Mesa Verde and the Sleeping Ute Mountain called Yucca House. This site represents one of the late sites in southwestern Colorado; it was inhabited in the time right before Pueblo people moved to new homes farther south, where present-day Pueblo people still live today. Yucca House also has a special connection to the Tewa-speaking Pueblos from whence it received its name.[1] As we stood on the top of the highest rubble mound in the center of Yucca House, we could see black rain clouds rolling over the top of Mesa Verde. The clouds were moving very quickly and seemed to be expanding. Within minutes lightning was flashing all around us and sent us back to our vehicles. We

Porter Swentzell describes spheres at Edge of the Cedars Museum.

headed back to Crow Canyon to set up camp, but ended up spending the night under the porch roof, because of torrential rain and a rare tornado. The ferocity of the storm almost seemed ominous.

I come from Santa Clara Pueblo, one of six Tewa-speaking Pueblos located in northern New Mexico. Santa Clara Pueblo, or Khap'o Owingeh, as it is known in Tewa, is one of the larger of the Tewa villages, with more than three thousand members. It sits on the western side of the Rio Grande at the mouth of the Santa Clara Canyon, which runs up into the Jemez Mountains. The current village was founded probably sometime in the sixteenth century, when a group of Tewas moved down into the valley from Púujeh Owingteji (Puye Cliff Dwellings) after centuries of living on the Pajarito Plateau. Shortly before or after they moved into the valley, the first encounters with Spanish explorers and treasure seekers took place. In 1598 Don Juan de Oñate established the first Spanish colony at Jungeh Owingeh, a few miles north of Santa Clara Pueblo. Spanish colonization created a crisis in Pueblo country of enormous proportions. Pueblo labor was harnessed to build missions in Pueblo villages, as Franciscan missionaries attempted to convert Pueblos to Christianity by all means available. Spanish secular government alternated between permitting Pueblo expressions of culture and ruthlessly crushing them. Meanwhile, demands for labor and tribute taxed the subsistence economy of Pueblo people, as they struggled to cope with waves of new diseases, famine, and increasing raids by traditional enemies. The Pueblo population fell precipitously. By 1680 most of the Pueblos had had enough. Santa Clara Pueblo joined its neighboring Pueblos in the famous revolt that ejected the Spanish from New Mexico for a half generation. Although the Spanish returned to New Mexico, the reactive explosion represented by the Pueblo Revolt ensured that the Pueblos would not face the same level of persecution they had faced under the first century and a half of contact with the Spanish. However, they would face further challenges to their land, language, and culture during the later Mexican and American periods.

The Spanish colonial government had provided certain protections for Pueblo people. In particular, the Spanish land grants given to each Pueblo ensured that each community's surrounding lands were protected from encroachment. These protections wilted after Mexico gained its independence and dried up further in the initial decades after the American invasion of the Southwest. While the US government eventually put a halt to most encroachment by non-Indians on Pueblo lands, they brought new threats to Pueblo culture. The Indian boarding-school system started by Captain Richard H. Pratt operated with the objective to "kill the Indian and save the man." Pueblo children were among those who were shipped to boarding schools, where all traces of language and culture were prohibited in the effort to turn them into "good Americans." Boarding schools were coupled with assimilationist policies in the hope of solving "the Indian problem," but results among the Pueblos were mixed. Pueblo people had continued to live in their centuries-old homes, speak their languages, and carry on their traditions. The strength of their communities had guided them through the storm of outside influences, but things began to change when the federal government eased its forceful policies and began to offer gifts to tribes. Low-income homes were offered, and Pueblo people embraced them as their ancient villages began to crumble. The gifts multiplied: free health care, free vocational training, and even free food. Good-paying jobs at Los Alamos National Laboratory, the Bureau of Indian Affairs, and the Indian Health Service allowed many Pueblo families to acquire the trappings of the modern American middle class.

As they gained these shiny new toys, they began to lose something more important. Language, the cornerstone of Pueblo culture and traditions, was slipping away. In 2005 the governor of Santa Clara Pueblo found that only one child out of three hundred could speak Tewa fluently. Television, computers, government housing, the wage economy, and materialism combined may represent some of the more dangerous threats that Pueblo culture has ever faced. They have accomplished in a few decades what centuries of European contact failed to do—cultural assassination by candy bar. In spite of these challenges, the Pueblo peoples of the Southwest have been fortunate to retain much of their traditional culture and their languages— especially in comparison to many other tribes around the United States. An increasing awareness of the loss of language and culture within Pueblo communities may stem the flow of cultural disintegration before it is too late. As a member of a Pueblo community, I am reminded that as Pueblo people, we must remember who we are and where we came from so that we can continue the work of those who came before us.

Our oral traditions trace our roots to pre-Columbian sites throughout the region. Tewa oral history begins with the emergence of the people from beneath a lake to the north. As the people began to move southward from the place of emergence, they were repeatedly required to turn back because they lacked some significant aspect of their culture. Each time they ventured forth, they became more complete, and when they were complete enough, they began their journey to our present locations. This journey did not take place quickly, because the people were moving southward with their elderly and children. Sometimes they would stop and build a village where they would live for a time. These places where they stopped are now recognized as the archaeological sites that are found throughout the Southwest. It is important to note that these "sites" are not merely "ruins." They are places where people lived for generations—places where people shed the strength of their arms, their legs, their breath, and their hearts. When people do that, they are forever a part of that place, no matter how much time has passed. The ground still murmurs with the treading of their feet, and the air carries the sounds of their voices and songs. Visiting these "ruins" must be conducted as though the occupants were still there—because they are.

These are the thoughts that I carry with me when I visit these places. I know that I exist only as a result of all those who have come before me. The things that they learned and passed on serve as the basis for our existence as Pueblo people today. It is with profound respect and gratitude that I visit these sites. I believe that the humility, respect, and care that one embodies while visiting can reward one in the same way that the rain has rewarded people in the Southwest for thousands of years. In the same way, a lack of these attributes could manifest itself in the form of a tornado, like the one that passed near Cortez on that first evening. As I lay trying to fall asleep on the hard cement porch at Crow Canyon, I wondered whether the unusual weather had anything to do with our initial meeting and visit to Yucca House. Maybe it was telling us to remember to be respectful.

That next morning, we set out to visit the Sand Canyon site. It was easy for me to slip into my "tour guide" persona in answering the first fusillade of questions. However, I was also still trying to wrap my mind around the goal of the project and exactly what these guys wanted. I needed to read these guys—especially the archaeologist (Steve Wolverton). As Pueblo people, we are constantly reminded by our elders about what we can and can't speak about. We are specifically advised not to speak about the content of religious ceremonies. This is a precaution that can be specifically traced back to the harsh persecution of Pueblo religion under Spanish priests and of the vocal disdain for Pueblo dances by later

Porter Swentzell offers his thoughts to Taylor and Wolverton at Butler Wash.

American missionaries. It is also something that is ingrained in us through our social system. One acquires knowledge as one advances through life. Knowledge is gender, age, and society specific. As a result, no one ever knows "everything," but those who have lived their whole lives as Pueblo people may know a great deal about some things. Knowledge should not be acquired through asking questions or reading a book but should be gained through long hours of careful observation, followed by trial and error. These ways of sharing knowledge have served and continue to serve to bind communities together, while perpetuating Pueblo core values of respect, caring, humbleness, and appreciation.

Porter Swentzell teaching students a Pueblo game at Crow Canyon Archaeological Center.

Over the past century, Pueblo peoples have been bombarded with inquisitive anthropologists, archaeologists, tourists, and New Agers who have sometimes violated this knowledge system, knowingly or unknowingly. Anthropologists and archaeologists as a class have acquired a reputation for seeking information in order to further their individual professional goals. Anthropologists who managed to infiltrate some Pueblos typically published the information they had managed to acquire, whether that information had been gathered ethically or more unscrupulously. The publication of content from within the Pueblo knowledge system disrupts the carefully designed socioreligious systems—now anyone could become privy to information that might take a Pueblo person decades of living within the community to learn. Also, someone who has only read about our culture has no experience in it and thus has not really learned it at all. Pueblo people have decried the publishing of this material for decades, but this cannot repair the damage already done. Published material is nearly impossible to "unpublish." At the same time, information given to anthropologists was sometimes published without the proper context and thus led to misconceptions about Pueblo people and culture. This interest in Pueblo people and culture has also led to its commodification—a

Porter Swentzell discusses interpretation of the site with rangers at Spruce Tree House.

process assisted in no small part by Pueblo people themselves. With commodification comes the idea that culture and people are somehow frozen in time rather than imbued with the vitality and dynamism that have always existed and continue to exist to the chagrin of many tourists.

This is the public side of the Pueblo-anthropologist interaction, but from a Pueblo perspective the consequences of spending too much time with archaeologists or anthropologists can be exceedingly dangerous. Edward S. Curtis recorded an account of a San Ildefonso Pueblo man who was apparently executed for speaking with anthropologist

Matilda Coxe Stevenson around 1913, and as recently as 1923 two Santo Domingo Pueblo men were executed for participating in an exhibition dance in Washington, DC.[2] To this day, those Pueblo people who acquire a reputation for talking with outsiders risk ostracism, loss of property, banishment, and even corporal punishment. As a result, I am always wary in the presence of anthropologists and archaeologists. I am always careful that the knowledge that is shared is appropriate and does not further damage the existing knowledge system. However, the dangers of simple association are very real and certainly remained in my mind as we drove to Sand Canyon.

On the first day with the team, I was surprised at how quiet Steve W. was—he didn't profess any knowledge about Sand Canyon other than a very general description of the site. I had half expected him to expound on all the information that I knew had been gathered by archaeologists over the years at Sand Canyon. Despite the variegated history of Pueblo-archaeologist interactions, I am interested in their theories and am particularly excited to see correlations between archaeological findings and oral traditions. It was clear that Steve W. was avoiding providing excessive context. After a few minutes of wandering around, Steve W. and I left David and Steve B. to "do their art thing." Steve B. found a prominent place to stand and take pictures, while David disappeared into the trees with his journal. Steve W. and I walked back to the parking lot and found a picnic table, where we sat down and started to talk. The gist of the project began to take shape as he described the other team members not yet there, Melinda Levin (a filmmaker) and Rob Figueroa (a philosopher). He talked about telling the story of Mesa Verde from a number of different and unconnected perspectives—an idea that still didn't make much sense to me at the time. I could understand how a Pueblo person and an archaeologist might end up spending time in the region, but why would we need a filmmaker, a photographer, a poet, or a philosopher? I decided to table my confusion. Instead of the standard Pueblo-archaeologist interaction, our conversation wandered to human health and moral responsibility. It was at this point that it began to dawn on me that this project was different. This would not be about "cultural interpretation" or about careful maneuvering to protect private cultural practices from prying questions. Instead, this would be a multilayered conversation between human beings with different backgrounds and perspectives about the world.

However, I still wasn't sure how this conversation would take place between a Pueblo person, an archaeologist, a poet, a photographer, a filmmaker, and a philosopher. But there were some clues. This trip and a future one would require long rides in crowded vehicles with plenty of downtime to talk about everything except the project. On the first trip we headed to Butler Wash, Utah, to visit an ancestral Pueblo site. As we were driving to Hovenweep National Monument on our return trip, we passed by fields of green alfalfa growing out of the stark desert. Somehow in our comments the term *astrofalfa* was coined in response to the unnatural sight of these fields. We joked that "astrofalfa" would be the miracle crop of the future that would provide the solution for any issue facing people. Whether it was soft drinks or tires, houses or animal feed, it could be made out of "astrofalfa." The joke grew exponentially from that point forward, as we developed new products, marketing campaigns, and even catchphrases, or "falfaisms." Despite the often juvenile level of some of the humor, it served to relax the barriers between the project members and created a common ground that overrode our disparate backgrounds. To me, "astrofalfa" also represented a critique of the superficiality, commodification, and placelessness that seem to be pervasive in much of today's world. I had to question my own role in this commodification—in particular the commodification of culture and place. I had agreed to meet with the group to provide cultural interpretation in exchange for money. Was I turning Pueblo culture and history into a form of "astrofalfa"? For the time being, "astrofalfa" seemed like it might be the only "product" from our first trip to the Mesa Verde region.

We returned to the area in October 2011, with the addition of Melinda and Rob. Our arrival coincided with another unusual storm bringing very cold weather to the area. We camped at Mesa Verde and set up our tents in the middle of a sleet storm. The temperatures were very cold for that time of year. Within a short period of time, we all became very focused on trying to stay warm rather than having interdisciplinary and intercultural discussions. I spent most of the trip wearing almost all the clothes that I brought with me layered on top of each other. The harshness of the weather served a similar role as humor had on the previous trip—it removed barriers. It was almost as if the weather had joined the discussion with the comment that our conceptions of self-importance, privacy, and comfort were not helpful and that we had better shed them if we planned on doing anything useful. Be humble! There was a certain

Astrofalfa fields as seen from the air.

point when our different levels of expertise became irrelevant and we
resorted to being a small group of humans huddled around a smoky fire.

Once barriers began to crumble and common ground to appear,
we could begin to do some "work." One of the most powerful aspects
of the Mesa Verde region is the place itself. Although I have visited the
area many times, I am always surprised at how striking the environment
is. Blue-green mountains encircle red and yellow mesas dotted with dark-
green piñon and juniper trees. Cliff dwellings tucked into sandstone for-
mations hint at millennia of human presence. It is a place full of place.
Cultural context is almost unnecessary, because the landscape tells the

Porter Swentzell and Steve Wolverton hike toward the horizon, Butler Wash.

story on its own. The ancient sites were placed within the landscape and molded to it—they are as much part of the landscape as the rocks, bushes, and trees. One is constantly reminded that the landscape is alive.

On our first trip to Butler Wash, Steve W. and I had decided to walk to the top of the sandstone bluff behind the cliff dwelling to see what was on the other side. We climbed to what appeared to be the top, only to discover that a higher rise lay behind it and another behind that. Almost magically, each time we climbed higher, another stretch of sandstone manifested itself. A cloud blotted out the sun, and the landscape suddenly felt foreboding. We turned back to find David and Steve B. lost in their work. Maybe the landscape was talking to them, too. They were busy observing it, listening to it, and feeling it. The sites and the landscape illustrated the contrast between the modern world of "astrofalfa" and the way that human beings have interacted with their environment for most of our existence.

During these first two trips, I had gotten a feeling for the team, our work, and our personalities—although words like *interdisciplinary project* still didn't mean too much to me. We had visited an area with which I was very comfortable and familiar, a place I had known since I was a little kid.

Porter Swentzell draws symbol for community/place in sand at Elm Fork
Education Exhibit Hall at University of North Texas.

We were visiting *my* ancestral home and thinking about *my* history. This is
not to say that these visits brought nothing new to my understanding of
the past. I was excited to see some of the ways my ancestors had devised
to survive or express themselves that I hadn't noticed before. However,
in hindsight this familiarity restricted my understanding of the project.
After all, I didn't know where the other team members came from or how
exactly they would tell the story of Mesa Verde through the framework of
an interdisciplinary project. Our next meeting would change much of this
for me.

In April 2012 we met up at the University of North Texas in Denton. The purpose was to present some of the experiences and work that had been completed by members of the team. Large versions of Steve B.'s photographs and David's poems were hung on the walls of the exhibit hall of the Environmental Education, Science, and Technology Building. Melinda created a short film filled with striking imagery, sounds, and quotes. The poems, photographs, and film each reflected aspects of the landscape, but they captured much more than that. They also captured human culture and our relationship with place. Although the media were different, they all seemed to be headed in a similar direction from different starting places. I kept seeing the contrast, so clearly evident in the Mesa Verde region, between the ancient human-landscape interaction and the modern human relationship with place. It was clear to me that our combined experiences together and in the same place had affected each of our perspectives in a similar way. We had experienced the region through respectful observation, and we had shared our perspectives from a place of humbleness. I felt that this had led us to care and appreciate each of the perspectives that we brought in a more profound way than if we had presented our experiences independently. Rob's presentation served as an "aha" moment for me, as he defined key terms like *integrated, interdisciplinary*, and *multidisciplinary*. I had received my bachelor's degree in integrated studies and was in a graduate program in interdisciplinary studies but had no idea what these terms meant—I actually thought they were just tools for universities to create degree programs when they lacked enough personnel to fill out a more standard degree program. It finally dawned on me that the work we were doing was more specialized than I originally thought and that the strange combination of our team had a logic to it that might make a lot of sense. This seemed very intuitive to me, because in many ways interdisciplinary work actually mirrors the Pueblo knowledge system—especially if it is done in the way that it is intended. This epiphany (for me) could also explain why each team member's perspective appeared to be heading in a similar direction.

My understanding of the work that we were doing was further expanded in the period after our primary meetings had taken place. In October 2012 I attended the Association of Integrated Studies (now the Association of Interdisciplinary Studies) conference in Oakland, Michigan. At the conference I spoke about some of my experiences participating in the Mesa Verde Project and was surprised at the response

Porter Swentzell offers his thoughts to Melinda Levin and park ranger at Spruce Tree House.

I received. There were many panels at the conference on the theory of interdisciplinarity, but few examples of applied practice. Many interdisciplinarians at the conference were excited to learn more about interdisciplinarity in the field—especially considering the makeup of our group. My colleagues from Northern New Mexico College were excited by the experience and began the process of creating a similar kind of interdisciplinary research team. In July 2013 I applied for and was selected for a faculty position in the Indigenous Liberal Studies program at the Institute of American Indian Arts in Santa Fe, New Mexico. After I was selected, I was told that a key part of the final decision was based on my "interdisciplinary background." These later events spoke to me about how special the Mesa Verde Project was and about the importance of interdisciplinarity in the larger world of academia. As a participant in the project, I had little thought about the life-changing events that would follow. Thoughts like these were far from my mind as I visited with Steve W., Steve B., Melinda, Rob, and David in Denton.

The trip to Denton was also very different from our first two meetings in the Mesa Verde region. Visiting Denton was outside of my usual realm of experience. I had visited Dallas before, but this was my first visit to Denton. Melinda, David, and Steve W. all played excellent hosts, as they showed me around Denton and around the University of North Texas campus. The generosity and hospitality they showed in opening their homes to me will last for a long time. David kindly showed me around the place where he grew up. The old town of Denton looked like it could belong in any western college town, but David pointed out the surrounding areas that were primarily agricultural lands when he was growing up. These fields now grew prefabricated buildings and car dealerships. I had seen similar things happen in New Mexico, but not nearly on the same scale.

The visit to UNT impacted me far more than the two visits to the Mesa Verde region because of the human environment of the Dallas–Fort Worth area. When I returned to Santa Clara Pueblo, I wrote an e-mail to the rest of the team:

> As I was leaving yesterday I was struck with a feeling of fear mixed with urgency. The endless rows of chain-restaurants interspersed with big-box stores looked not only formidable, but also unstoppable. As the plane banked over urban sprawl, my eyes were caught by the turquoise glitter of all the backyard swimming pools. Landing in New Mexico, I felt afraid for my homeland.
>
> Chain-restaurants, big-box stores, and urban sprawl are not unique to any particular place. Each place also has its own versions of used-bookstores, backyard beer gardens, and Cuban bakeries. However, seeing such an overt flexing of corporate power is rare for me. In Santa Clara Pueblo I can ignore many issues with relative ease. I am not used to being in a place where these issues are tenaciously present. I am left pondering what our endgame as human beings is.

The contrast between Dallas and New Mexico was sharp. The contrast between Dallas and the Mesa Verde region was shocking. I began to realize what was so important about our group and the exchange of perspectives, the sharing of space, and the breakdown in barriers that we had experienced. We could begin to speak to each other from a place of honesty rather than relying on our professional personae. Despite my pontificatory e-mail, I too am a participant in the greater commodification of the world. I must become more aware of the role that I play in the destruction of those things that we hold dear. Aside from the hours spent laughing, sleeping, or trying to stay warm, we were doing something very serious, important, and arguably fundamentally human. We could grow as human beings (both collectively and individually) from the experience of sharing our different perspectives.

Regardless of our cultural backgrounds or what part of the world we live in, we are all human beings who are the result of all those who came before us. Just as their actions led us to where we are today, our actions lay the path for all that will ever exist from this moment forward. This perspective of the world is a part of the principles that guided Pueblo peoples for countless generations and still carries us forward in many ways today. There were times when we deviated from these principles in the past, but the consequences of such deviation were always remembered. The endless expanses of subdivisions and rampant materialism seem to be a deviation on a monumental scale. It dwarfs any deviations that occurred centuries ago in the Four Corners region. Perhaps we are reaching the final stage as humans that Max Weber eloquently summarized: "Specialists without spirit, sensualists without heart; this nullity imagines that it has attained a level of civilization never before achieved."[3] In a sense, the consumerism is akin to irrigating alfalfa in the middle of the desert. The incredible amount of water required to grow alfalfa in such an arid environment is a poor use of such a precious resource. It lays a path for the future that forfeits all who come after us in the name of short-term progress.

I would like to think that we have not quite reached such a soulless place of self-importance. Maybe this is what makes interdisciplinary projects like ours so crucial. There may be fear and danger for those coming from different disciplines or backgrounds in collecting together, but if a place of respect can be established, these obstacles can be overcome. Once they are overcome, it is vital to nurture an environment of humbleness and empathy. Then maybe, through nonadversarial sharing, we can appreciate our differences but also grow from each other's perspectives. This may be part of what is necessary to keep our world from completely falling into the dystopic world that Weber imagined. It is not a simple suggestion or a guaranteed solution, but it helps to raise our awareness of each other, of other places, and of our purpose as humans. Hopefully, it reminds us to think about how we decide to lay the path for those who come after us.

NOTES

1. Scott G. Ortman, *Winds from the North: Tewa Origins and Historical Anthropology* (Salt Lake City: University of Utah Press, 2012), 185–87.

2. Edward S. Curtis, *The Tiwa. The Keres*, vol. 16 of *The North American Indian* (Norwood, MA: Plimpton Press, 1926), 163–65.

3. Max Weber, *The Protestant Ethic and the Spirit of Capitalism*, translated by Talcott Parsons (1930; reprint, London: Routledge Classics, 2010), 124.

5

Location/Fracture
Documentary Storytelling in Mesa Verde

Melinda Levin

As a documentary film director and theorist, I often interact and collaborate with others who take me outside of my proverbial comfort zone, whether these be Mayan farmers, homeless veterans, paramilitary officers, American cattle ranchers, or Hezbollah fighters. I'm pretty cool with being uncomfortable and tested; most documentary filmmakers are. The intense curiosity and adrenaline of telling a story about humanity and our planet help one stay focused and artistic in the face of physical and emotional difficulties. The challenges the Mesa Verde Project presented to me were not dangerous, but subtle and wonderfully subversive, both personally and in terms of my role as an environmental documentary film director. The documentary director must remain malleable and open to abrupt change, but does come to a project with a clear sense of likely outcomes and stated goals. Our team objective to "go to the field together" and to look and create through multiple lenses at once was more procedural than content related, which was unique in my experience. My efforts with this team are part of a longer-term trajectory of rethinking my own work, the role of universities in a state of flux, and a planet under vast pressure.

As a part-time resident of the region that the Mesa Verde Ancestral Puebloans lived in, I feel that I have a personal stake in this story. I come from European lineage, from a group of restless English, French, German, and Irish farmers, weavers, porters, and Anglican vicars who migrated west across a vast ocean. While my paternal grandmother, who was born in Oklahoma Indian Territory, told me that we had Cherokee in our blood, I am not obviously from an indigenous culture. But I will

Melinda Levin at the University of North Texas presentation. Photograph by Alicia Taylor.

very likely play out a good part of my life within a geographic arm's reach of where the Mesa Verde civilization thrived and eventually departed, and I am now a small part of the deep history of this beautiful and challenging area. I build memories, tradition, and hopes here. I don't assume to tell "the story of Mesa Verde," but rather "a story of Mesa Verde." That story, it turns out, is only tangentially archaeological. Instead, what is Mesa Verde depends on one's heritage, one's vantage point, and even perhaps the company one is in.

So I come to this project, and as part of this team, as someone who is intrigued with how I can make a film about a culture that literally no longer exists in the same manner. Many modern descendants of these Ancestral Puebloans, including a member of our research team, now live farther south, near the Rio Grande. But the impressive and evocative rise and collapse of a vast community haunts me with similarities of present-day environmental, agricultural, and self-identity challenges worldwide, including in this corner of the United States. I see a few too many parallels in terms of drought, external forces impacting successful agricultural practices, foreign species invasion, and the sustainability of cultural traditions. These challenges and our human response to them make a good story.

Coalescing in the Classroom

While in my own documentary film work I spend substantial time on content research in the months or years leading up to production in the field, our team started a practice early on that was new to me, and in the process extraordinarily helpful. In addition to reading research and more informal meetings over coffee, lunch, or beer, we established weekly meetings to present the basics of our own academic fields to each other. Steve Wolverton, David, Rob, and I were in Texas. Porter was in New Mexico, and Steve Bardolph was in Minnesota, so they joined these meetings by videoconference. At each meeting, one of us would take the proverbial podium in a classroom reserved for our team. It was summertime, and more than once I saw people walking down the hall give confused looks at our group of professors walking into the classroom armed with computers, but no students. These teaching sessions allowed us to prime each other on the basic terminology, history, experiences, and perceptions of our wildly divergent fields. In a sense, we were becoming novice apprentices to each other. Steve Wolverton presented first, and I vividly remember the excitement in the room as the rest of us got a firmer grasp of not only archeological concepts and the deep history of the Mesa Verde region we would be heading into, but perhaps more important the passion, grace, and commitment of our colleague and friend. David Taylor walked us through the controversial history of ethnopoetics and his reemerging interest in its approaches and uses. Steve Bardolph shared a fantastic, condensed history of his landscape photographic work, beginning with museum-quality single-image pictures to multiple-image, mathematically captured and presented tableaus of a location that provided an energetic, moving re-presentation of place. Robert Figueroa and Porter Swentzell discussed environmental justice, indigenous rights, and issues of heritage, culture, and memory.

I talked a bit about my scholarship, peer-reviewed publications, grants, awards, and the like. But more to the point for our work, I presented my interests in the impact of tourism and the Mesa Verde region's ongoing role as a migration corridor (by people and wildlife and more recently under a transnational airline flyway). I also offered what I hoped would be a grounded definition of "documentary" as opposed to "journalism," with some indication of my particular interests in the Mesa Verde region, including conflicting truths and issues of "truth" versus "reality." I am familiar with teaching these ideas, terms, and processes to those in my own field, but had a vague sense of vulnerability relaying them to our research team members. It was almost as if I were giving away trade secrets possibly better left in my private toolbox. But since my colleagues had emptied out their own bags of tricks for the betterment of the team, I did my best to articulate these challenges and broad definitions of my field. I went into this collaboration with a transparent mind-set and a willingness to expose, or at least to identify, my own tendencies and challenges.

The opportunity to learn from and collaborate with people of this caliber is a rare privilege, so none of us took our group lightly as we slowly began coalescing as a "research team." We challenged each other and strategized as to how best to mesh our practices and intentions. These presentations and the discussions afterward allowed us to reflect on each of our roles in developing a cohesive group with immense respect for our varied fields.

Traditional "Return on Investment" Pressures in Higher Education

Steve Wolverton states in his chapter that the pressure for a firmly articulated return on investment is a fundamental expectation in funded academic research, and I agree that our lack of a specific goal—other than to "go into the field and see what happens"—was at times uncomfortable for all of us.

Universities understandably thrive on national and international recognition, on government and development definitions of what it means to be a "research institution," and on strong connections with industry and large funding entities. If there is not substantial funding, interdisciplinary research can be seen as "pie in the sky" impractical work. As a former university department chair myself, I can vouch for the ROI indoctrination of administrators at all levels. Formal "research clusters," a current interdisciplinary trend that establishes formal ties between faculties of different fields, still often require massive federal funding infusion to retain validity and support in the eyes of upper administration and for public institutions or government officials.

Traditional ROI requires clearly stated goals and foreseeable outcomes up front. While that is a logical template, I firmly believe that such external pressures can hinder creative thinking in STEM, humanities, arts, business, social science, and other fields. This Mesa Verde team collaboration freed up some of these constraints for each of us and opened us up to a more holistic, organic, valid platform for truly interdisciplinary research and results.

As a nascent team, we had early discussions about a wide variety of physical locations for research, including the escarpment of the Andes in western Argentina, the Chesapeake Bay, and others. We decided on Mesa Verde for several reasons, including the fact that several of us were familiar with the region and its relative geographical proximity for several of the team members, as well as overall interests in combining arts with science research, indigenous rights and social justice, and location-based documentation opportunities. However, the physical location was not as important as the team and the collaboration.

Once we agreed on a large site of research, we brought on key team member Porter Swentzell and set out toward our stated ROI: "to go into the field and see what happens." As visual artists, perhaps Steve Bardolph and I were the most at ease with this uncertain goal, but for me the lack of a clear "documentary narrative" and my hesitation to prod too deeply into indigenous knowledge and traditions did prompt a vague lack of direction at times. How does one tell a story of a physical place with conflicting stories? This and my concern about offending those who held conflicting stories of

Mesa Verde heritage were to be some of my challenges. Location, heritage, and narrative, all wrapped in tenuous uncertainty—this was hardly a traditional research process for documentary filmmaking. Commitment to collaboration and exploration was to become the glue of this project because there was nothing else to hinge on. This flies in the face of contemporary convention concerning "how to do" productive research, yet that thread is the very thing missing from much of what we do.

ALL TOGETHER, IN THE FIELD

My first moment with all six members of our core research team was during a balmy October afternoon in a Cortez, Colorado, Super Wal-Mart. Five of us (Steve Bardolph, Rob Figueroa, David Taylor, Steve Wolverton, and I) had flown into Durango from Denver that day and rented a van. Porter Swentzell drove up from New Mexico to meet us. While the rest of us scurried about for basic camp food and water, Porter arrived in his truck. Rob and I had not been on the first Mesa Verde summer location trip, so this was the first time the entire core team was physically together.

Colorado was in the final throes of an extended Indian summer that had brought mild days and sunshine. The Weather Channel told us that afternoon would bring a cold front from the Pacific Northwest, with quickly dropping temperatures, driving winds, rain, and snow at the higher elevations. In the interest of time, we agreed to break up shopping lists. David, Porter, and I headed to the "Outdoor" section, where I grabbed a big box of hand warmers and extra socks. Prior to heading to Colorado from Texas, I had bought a one-person North Face tent and had also packed my old, small "camping pillow." On one of the store aisles, I found pillows on sale for $2.99. We agreed that high-elevation tent camping with actual bedroom pillows would improve things immensely and tossed six pillows into the cart. Late that afternoon we made camp, built a fire, ate some food, smoked cigars (Wolverton thought that was a good idea), made final preparations for the next day, and headed to our tents in the dark and rapidly dropping temperatures.

I awoke in the middle of the night. Even inside my heavy sleeping bag, with a shirt, sweater, coat, hat, and gloves on, it was frigid. I thought I heard what sounded like a moose rubbing up against the outside of the tent, occasionally scraping the nylon with its hooves. I laid there for the longest time, slightly disoriented and trying to gauge the distance from my tent to those of my colleagues. In the end, in a rare instance when I recognized that I was the sole female and also least-experienced camper on the team, I bucked it up, assumed the moose would meander off (they're vegetarians, right?), and finally dozed off again.

The next morning, as I staggered out into the frigid, dark gray and wet morning, I saw David working to restart the campfire. I asked him if he heard the moose walking through camp and trying to get into my tent. I looked around, but there were no moose hoofprints in the mud. Only later would I learn that there are no moose in this part of the country. With a familiar, dry smile, David told me that it had sleeted most of the night, and the winds were blowing my tent pretty hard. "And by the way . . . do you know that you have a summer tent?"

"NAMING" OUR COLLABORATION: ACADEMIC BUZZWORDS

Any discussion of field-based, collaborative research involving scholars from different scholarly fields should offer some definition of basic academic buzzwords used and indicate the contexts for work of this nature. For our Mesa Verde research team, these terms are *multidisciplinary*, *interdisciplinary*, *interagency*, and *transdisciplinary scholarship*. It should be noted that we specifically did not use these terms to define ourselves or outwardly analyze the depth with which we invested in them.

These catchphrases are used by administrators and faculty alike, and the basic intentions of "breaking down silo walls" are often admirable. One can earn an advanced "interdisciplinary" degree, funding entities champion "multidisciplinary" tactics, and enlightened university administrators speak of reaching beyond the ivory towers of the academy with "transdisciplinary" and "interagency" approaches and projects. Yet these terms are often misunderstood and, while tacitly supported, run headlong into the orthodoxy of academic boundaries and the pressures of "preparing our students for the workforce."

At a basic level, *multidisciplinary* work draws strengths from various disciplines but stays within the boundaries of each collaborator's own scholarly field. Scholars come together to address a common area from their own field of expertise. I believe that our team definitely incorporated the tenets of a multidisciplinary approach.

In philosophy and sociology, the term *agency* is the capacity for a human to make choices and enact these choices and decisions within the world. Following this line of thinking, *interagency* is the interrelatedness of participatory intentions. Active interagency requires us to share an intention and act it out with others. In our team's scholarship, particularly in the field and from diverse academic bases, this interagency emerged from profound levels of curiosity, humility, and no small amount of humor. We had to be flexible, open to uncertainties, able to accept challenges to our own long-held disciplinary beliefs, and willing to push forward both individually and as a team. I believe this was a level at which the Mesa Verde group excelled. Wit and respect were pervasive throughout our preparations and fieldwork and prompted deeper levels of analysis.

Interdisciplinary work analyzes, synthesizes, and harmonizes links between disciplines into a coherent whole and often founds new areas of scholarship and application. One uses the tools, devices, and history of a different discipline while still retaining one's own grounding, traditions, and applications. Examples could be political science borrowing from economics, cinema borrowing lighting and color principles from painting, or environmental philosophy drawing from hydrology. Documentary cinema is almost by definition an interdisciplinary endeavor, so I have no problem claiming this one at some level as well.

Transdisciplinary work pushes boundaries even further and can be hazardous to the career of the unestablished scholar. In our group, we had a full professor, two associate professors, an assistant professor (now a tenured associate professor), a full-time senior lecturer, and a Tewa graduate student scholar (now an assistant professor himself!). Working not only across disciplinary borders but also traversing "ranks" within the academy allowed us to recognize, analyze, and discuss very real challenges of this type of scholarship. Truly transdisciplinary scholars integrate the practices of an entirely different field, some of these nonacademic fields, in a way that transcends traditional boundaries and expectations. A cell biologist teaching her field through poetry or a costume designer through field anthropology would indicate transdisciplinary pedagogy. Similarly, research would take the practitioner out of the realm of traditional scholarship and into an entirely new arena. One can be seen as essentially "abandoning" your home department and academic degrees and using whatever tools necessary that you are able to master to engage your field at a new, possibly more profound level. Our group delicately entered the realm of transdisciplinarity, and I suspect our further work will move deeper into this arena.

Transdisciplinary work often aims to acknowledge and even call out the hierarchical relationship between researchers and those being researched. It is important to avoid ethno- or academy-centric biases and to retain an open mind. While a power imbalance may still exist, transparent and articulated intentions (even if those are simply working in the field together) can bring the local context into full influence. The possibility of such vulnerability for successful participants working at the "top of their game" is critical, and I believe it depends on the personalities involved. Assessing these tendencies early on is key to forming a successful transdisciplinary partnership. For our team, these academic buzzwords are mostly post hoc descriptions that others use to categorize the holistic work we are doing. We understand that collegiality, collaboration, and relationships valued ahead of anticipated products allow us to stand on long-held and deep expertise in new settings with success and productivity. Perhaps we are the "anticluster" cluster. Perhaps these terms for our team are simply ways of being, not benchmarks to achieve.

Brittle Landscape, Time, and Stories

The "brittleness" of the larger story of Mesa Verde makes it both fascinating and frustrating for me as a filmmaker. It became clear that while I could produce a successful "traditional" documentary with interviews, observational footage of archaeological sites, statistics, and a classic narrative arc, this approach was not going to lead my intentions. At least not for the moment. What I needed to do on location more than anything was observe and listen. My camera did not come out much early while on location with the team, which is unusual for me.

The landscape in the Mesa Verde region changes wildly from sage-covered, dry high desert to snow-capped peaks. The arroyos and washes can reach temperatures above one hundred degrees in the summertime, and blizzards are not uncommon in the winter. What is fairly constant is the brittleness of the land. Winds, relative lack of precipitation, loamy soil, and land erosion result in delicate, arid, and difficult agricultural conditions. Whether this climate impacted the radical changes in the Mesa Verde civilization depends on who is telling the story. Some scholars claim soil degradation, drought, and other human-made environmental stressors prompted massive societal changes. Some historians purport that internal clashes, intercommunity warfare, extreme social trauma, religious conflict, or some combination of these caused die-offs and migration. While his discussions with us were nuanced and complex, at a basic level Porter posited that it was simply time for these communities to physically and spiritually move on; thus, they left.

Melinda Levin sits with the group at Butler Wash.

In my work in environmental and social-issue documentary, I have heard people from vastly different walks of life and very different regions of the world speak of understanding their location through deep time. One cattle rancher I know in Colorado has termed this practice "becoming native to your environment" and believes this is a multigenerational process. Many people tether the idea of respect to this purpose and experience "becoming native" in profound and layered ways.

When our team was on-site at the Butler Wash archaeological site in southern Utah, Porter told us that in his way of thinking, it is important to respect a thing before attempting to understand it. He noted that while

Melinda Levin films at Butler Wash.

most scholars strive to analyze and "know" something before offering it respect, it appeared that our team was bucking that trend and striving to respect these locations, histories, and traditions without even fully "understanding" them. I will venture to say that hearing this and acknowledging that "respect before knowledge" was our intention was one of our proudest moments as a team, one that anchored us from that point on. As a successful, tenured full professor, it was an odd relief to have this intention acknowledged. It also called to my attention the temporal, locational, and psychologically layered nature of "understanding" a place or thing and the time required to get to that understanding or knowledge.

We were shedding our fretful desire to predict return on investment and were embracing our desperate need for creativity, seemingly forgotten in the recesses of youth. Porter had given us permission and encouragement to do so.

THE CAMERA

While film gear is more portable than ever, it still takes up more space and is harder to lug into the field than the devices of the poet or the Tewa expert. With no additional film crew members, my Mesa Verde collaborators quickly earned the title "production assistants" and helped me carry various items into remote locations and up perilous cliff-dwelling ladders. David also volunteered to become "second unit camera" at the Butler Wash site and scurried down a cottonwood canyon to gather silent shots of the green, wet landscape below the dry high-mesa dwellings I was filming. I brought a high-definition video camera as well as a small Super-8 film camera, with the intention of mixing imagery from both. One would give crisp, professional deep-focus shots, while the other would record softer, compressed depth-of-field and "home movie"–appearing images. A "dolly track," carefully laid on sandstone cliffs or in the middle of a remote highway, would allow me to acquire professional-looking, smooth moving images from a low angle, emphasizing foreground and spatial discrepancies on location.

Given the particulars of this project, and my intention to not make a "talking-head interview" film with archaeologists, park rangers, and indigenous scholars, I looked to a famous quote by Dziga Vertov that claims obvious construction in the documentary genre: "I am eye. I am a mechanical eye. I, a machine, am showing you a world, the likes of which only I can see."

This citation clearly marks the line between pure journalism and artistic documentary. In my Mesa Verde research, on location and in postproduction editing, I gathered information, visuals, sounds, perceptions, shadows, fears, and joys and presented the story I saw emerge over time spent in the Mesa Verde region. I had made extensive notes of comments, perceptions, and questions of my colleagues and used these, as well as my own observations, to guide my selection of locations, shot compositions, audio, and other cinematic elements. The basic challenges we had on location as a team are nothing new, nothing groundbreaking for academia, cinema, literature, or other arts. But in our case with Mesa Verde, with archaeologists and indigenous scholars as part of our peripheral and core team, it was important to me to allow those voices from "behind the scenes" to influence and ultimately enter my field of documentary perception. We were dealing with the science of archaeology and the "sacred" and tightly held precedents of historical categorization. We were also perhaps tampering with Native rights, traditions, spirituality, and history. We were dealing with an indigenous culture that most of us are not steeped in. The developing story required us to take risks. We were taking risks telling it.

Wolf Koenig said about documentary film, "Every cut is a lie. It's never that way. Those two shots were never next to each other in time that way. But you're telling a lie in order to tell the truth." So the idea of the truth, which is now considered by many to be a dried-out argument, is still one that I as a collaborative artist-scholar often wrestle with. Whose truth? Why the truth? Does it matter? To whom? What's the difference? It is all the difference in the world.

We are socialized and educated to structure, analyze, label, partition, and evaluate the world we live in, particularly if our intentions are scholarly in nature. But these tendencies actually form very early in life and help us navigate the world. We frame the world through our preconceived impulses in order to negotiate the vast amount of information provided. We often define things through binary comparisons: this is this, that is that, this is not that. Labeling and evaluative tendencies quickly follow. I clearly had ideas and opinions about Mesa Verde but on location did work hard to suppress them and listen.

As a documentary film director who easily slips into the tendencies and methods of a visual anthropologist, I had some uncomfortable moments during the early stages in the field for our Mesa Verde collaboration. Ethnographic and anthropological documentary directors are known to play the role of the "outsider making friends," open and accepting of local ways, socializing, developing some level of friendship, as at ease with casual conversation as more formal "interviews." I was at times painfully aware of the field tactic of socializing as a way of gathering information and creating rapport. This discomfort happened with my team members, the archaeologists we visited, and even with the National Park Service staff. I consider myself a self-aware and ethical scholar, artist, and person, but because of my natural curiosity, I had never before felt a pervasive tension with these tactics. I was caught off-guard by the awkward feeling of asking questions.

Melinda Levin and others listen to Porter Swentzell behind the wall at
Spruce Tree House.

In hindsight, I believe I was more uncomfortable than normal with
my visual anthropology tendencies on this project because I truly believed
that there was something different going on during our Mesa Verde fieldwork. While on prior films and research collaborations I had offered to
open myself up and answer any questions from my "subjects" themselves,
and developed a fondness that went beyond scholarly research, with this
team we began to easily drift into conversations that offered personal
information and engaged with others' perceptions of our own biases,
interpretations, personalities, and intentions. Perhaps prior to working

with this group I had reached a certain basic and often accepted level of scholarly cynicism. But this team had unexpectedly become the one that most challenged me and most deepened my curiosity. There was a kind of symbiosis among our team members that I had never experienced; the humor, sharing, and humanity among fellow academics were inspiring. Perhaps *because* of our dedication to simply work in the field together, we reached a new level of scholarship. The borders were taken down, and we were open to multiple levels of "truth" and "ownership." My tendencies toward the tenets of visual anthropology and documentary questioning dissolved into a much more organic, human curiosity.

LOCATION/FRACTURE

In my case, the imprecise and elusive nature of documenting an "abandoned location" and my artistic instinct in this situation to steer away from a traditional documentary approach prompted me, at least in the first incarnation of a Mesa Verde film, to consider fragmented visuals, sounds, memories, and stories as my key storytelling devices. My approach became much less "journalistic" and much more avant-garde in nature.

Indeed, the title of the first film to come out of this collaboration is *Location/Fracture*. This play on words indicates the occasionally abusive nature of physical archaeology to a site (digging, moving, breaking up), but also the divisive nature of perception, storytelling, and memory when it comes to place and culture. This film begins with sounds, which became extremely important to my own perception of this geographic place as well as to my understanding of the stakeholders involved. The audio of digging, hammering, and then the voices of tourists come in. As we look at the purposely shaky, moving footage of petroglyph symbols high on a desert wall, the tourists wonder aloud at what these images mean. We see ancient painted handprints, animals, spirals, and birds. The tourist voices wind in and out of the wind, and then disappear. The audio of a child's music box fades as we continue looking at this ancient set of stories. After a moment, the audience recognizes the song, "It's a Small World (After All)."

Wind, coyote howls, "Native" drums, and New Age musical compositions transition us to images of rocks piled up on prayer mounds in the desert. Even though they are now absent, tourists have left their mark, crafted small monuments to the spirit, and moved on.

Throughout this nine-minute film, quotes appear on-screen. These are actual things I heard while we were on location and serve to anchor

Petroglyphs along a trail at Mesa Verde.

the tendencies of the different stakeholders involved. The first was riffed off by team member Robert Figueroa, in part based on a comment I had made in my classroom presentation to the group the prior summer. As we drove in the van toward one of the archaeological sites that cold October, Robert said, "People have expectations of globalism when they come as tourist to these ancient sites. For example, we are probably going to eat sushi down in Cortez, Colorado, tonight."

I have long been interested in the deep intertwining of cultural identities in the American Southwest. In the Mesa Verde region, these currently include ranchers and corporate farmers, downwardly mobile

Melinda Levin discusses her film at Elm Fork Education Exhibit Hall at University of North Texas.

homesteaders, indigenous communities, religious recluses, mining and natural gas companies, winter and summer sports start-ups, micro brew-pubs, and tourists.

The idea of tourists as key stakeholders in the Mesa Verde region was one that piqued my curiosity early on; in fact, I talked about this in my aforementioned team presentation. The fact that I could sleep in a cold North Face tent or in a foreign-owned hotel, eat from a global menu, wear hiking boots made in China, softly meander through an ancient and sacred site, buy Wal-Mart pillows made in Taiwan, pay for my flight on a MasterCard, and fill our rental van with fuel from the North Sea is obviously now normal, but also classically and worrisomely postmodern, with tinges of hypermodernity.

In fact, while on location, Porter said to us all, "There's an odd idea now that you should be able to relate to anything, that we have the right to relate to any culture, any place, live anywhere in the world, any way we want." In a sense, as scholar-tourists, no matter how worthy and humble our intentions were, this is more or less what we were doing. We were taking the theories, histories, intentions, and ideas of various disciplines and cultures and looking at them together as a team. We were constructing a mash-up.

Cliff Palace at Mesa Verde.

I took it as my role to cinematically claim this, looking not only at the Mesa Verde region and the local stakeholders, but also at what we, as pretty high-level academic scholars and artists, were doing. On location, we were all grappling with this. In the film, I included a quote by Steve Wolverton, caught on tape during an informal conversation:

> As archaeologists, it's hard to stand back and say, "it's okay that we don't have the answers." We believe we can get the answers to anything. Why do you think we are so fascinated with a history that is not our own? Probably because U.S. history is an amalgam of cut-off histories.

During a solo research trip I had taken to Mesa Verde National Park about a month before our team endeavor, I bought tickets to two back-to-back one-hour National Park ranger tours of the Cliff Palace site. This location is perhaps one of the best-known and most photographed cliff-dwelling sites in the United States and has been visited now for decades by curious tourists. Quotes from these two different guides, who showed and explained the exact same site, were included in the film *Location/Fracture*:

10:00am Cliff Palace Tour, Park Ranger (Female): "This group was peaceful and agrarian. The children had the responsibility for taking care of the village dogs and turkeys. We have no archaeological evidence of violence."

11:00am Cliff Palace Tour, Park Ranger (Male): "The Cliff Palace residents were violent and aggressive toward other Mesa Verde communities nearby. It is human nature to be war-like."

I was also very interested in human use of symbols to make sense of place, our community, and ourselves. The petroglyph drawings are visible histories of decisions, observations, movement, and actions. One must know the "language" of these symbols to understand the stories told. Now, under a transcontinental flight corridor, one can look up from the ancient Cliff Palace site and see high-altitude jets. White airplane contrails are presented in the film, over the voice of a Federal Aviation Administration tower operator from LaGuardia Airport, talking to pilots. He uses secret symbols to convey information: "Mike, Alpha, November, Oscar, X-Ray, Sierra, Uniform, Bravo, Alpha, Lima . . . and standby . . ."

While fairly remote, the Butler Wash cliff dwelling in Utah has a sign with information about the area and a small fence to keep tourists from falling into the canyon below. Cinematically and personally, it was important to me to claim Porter's guidance to us, his graceful accommodation of our attempts to understand his historical "homeland." I included something he said to Steve Wolverton and me while we were sitting on a sloping cliff wall at this archaeological site:

> Just something as simple as that fence and sign, they alter your relationship in the landscape; you get an artificial view. In order to even start to understand this place, you have to go sit over there, or over here, and look at the moving clouds. Go sit over there and wait. You may get a bit of understanding.

Just after I incorporated this quote in the film, I included fast-motion footage of a tourist couple, bundled up in the early October cold, walk into the "off-limits" part of a small hilltop archeological site. They clearly move into areas they should not, take a few uncommitted pictures, and move on. They seem mildly impatient and going through the motions of "archaeological tourism." They were consuming the ruins. Soon after, the film transitions to footage taken through the windshield of a moving car,

Melinda Levin films on cliff edge at Butler Wash.

winding down the highway toward a sunrise in the East. Exotic "Indian" (East Asian) sitar music plays. We cut to a shot of a concrete slab where an old gas station used to sit; now weeds and trash surround it. The music fades, and wind and coyote howls come in. That was Indian music, right? This is an American archaeological site, is it not? Questions, assumptions, and confusion about place and time claim the upper hand in this section of the film.

TRUST, OPENNESS

I visited Porter a few months after our team visit to Mesa Verde. It was summer, during one of Santa Clara Pueblo's many feast days, and I was honored to join his extended family, including his wife, children, mother, sister, aunts, and uncle, at his grandmother's home. A communal home-cooked, traditional meal was offered, and his neighbors, other family, and friends came in and out of the house to share food and conversation. The day was long and hot, and there were several traditional dances being performed by those of the Summer Clan of Santa Clara. Porter is of the Winter Clan, so while he clearly and deeply knew the specific meanings and histories of these dances, he was able to stay close by to answer questions I quietly tossed his way in between the dances.

At one point, standing in the dirt plaza, waiting for the buffalo dancers and drummers to emerge from a building, I noticed a very nondescript, small hole in the ground. While it had a few feathers sticking out of it, it was otherwise almost unnoticeable, and I likely would not have seen it had I not been standing where I was for several minutes. This hole was not in the center of the plaza, but just a few feet to the right of the front door of an old, small adobe house. It seemed very random, and no one but me was paying it any attention. I leaned over to Porter and asked what it was. He paused for a moment, clearly gauging his words. For a moment, I regretted asking the question and quickly said, "Don't tell me something I should not know." What I meant to communicate was "I understand there are boundaries, and I think my question just crossed one." Porter gave a very respectful, small smile, leaned in, and said, "It is the center of the world. Be careful and don't step on it."

A few months prior, while up in the Mesa Verde region with our research team, Porter had told us about the emergence of his people through a hole into the current world and indicated that it may soon be time for another emergence and shift. A "reset," he called it.

I looked back over at this small hole in the ground, at the sweaty kids shuffling around, at the dust, and I started hearing the drums and singing begin. I could smell bread cooking somewhere nearby. The center of the world was about twelve feet away from me, simply and appropriately a part of the community. Dancers, drummers, and tourists mulled about. I wondered if this was the emergence spot from the previous world into this one. It was clearly marked to those in the know, but seemed equally a part of organic, familiar daily life. The idea of a "reset" is a wonderfully curious one to me—a concept that is at once beautifully inviting in its simplicity and challenging in its enormity.

A Journey

In classic mythology, from both the East and the West, there is a template often recognized within storytelling tropes. It is referred to in a number of different ways, but the most common moniker is Joseph Campbell's "hero's journey." This model is often reviewed and discussed in basic narrative writing and film courses at the undergraduate level. The tenets of certain stories can be very complex, and this controversial model certainly does not apply to all well-told tales. I bring this contentious and debatable model up not necessarily to promote it or challenge it (that has been accomplished by scores of other scholars and authors), but to recognize that as maladroit as it may sound, it provides a visual template to view my experience to date with our Mesa Verde team.

The hero's journey "monomyth" has been challenged, mimicked, written off as academic fluff, and labeled a technique that waters down, generalizes, and genderizes storytelling to very basic, noncomplex points of reference. The model is subverted in films such as *Dune* and *Chinatown*, where the "hero" may grow slightly but not dynamically alter in his original intent. Having said that, it is easily recognized in the stories and lives of Siddhartha, Jesus Christ, Odysseus, and Jonah. It can also be analyzed in the films *Rain Man*, *The Whale Rider*, *Beasts of the Southern Wild*, *The Wizard of Oz*, *Lord of the Rings*, *Slumdog Millionaire*, and other global cinema productions and tales. The message seems to be that growth is inevitable, perhaps painful, and that uncertainty cannot be escaped; humans are time lines as much as we are individuals. Time is illusory, but the past anchors into each of us as much as the future presents a horizon.

The diagram below indicates some of the formal markers or devices that the "hero's journey" archetype presents within wildly divergent stories and experiences over time.

While I don't necessarily think we are heroes in the common sense, I do recognize that the Mesa Verde research team purposely put ourselves at the upper right hand of the circle and for the most part, though perhaps without visibly dramatic death and rebirth, proceeded around this circle individually and as a team. The Ordinary World could be identified as our classic, scholarly silos and the Special World our experiences with transagency and inter-, multi-, and transdisciplinary work in the field

The Hero's Journey of Archetypal Storytelling

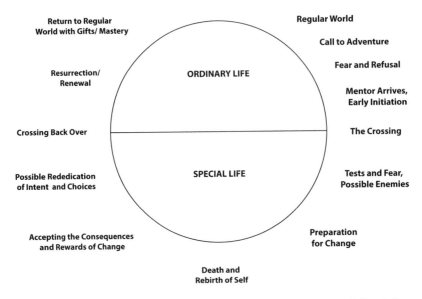

Adapted from the writings of Joseph Campbell in *The Hero's Journey: Joseph Campbell on His Life and Work* (Novato, CA: New World Library, 2014). Derived from Chris Vogler's version, found at http://www.thewritersjourney.com/hero's_journey.htm.

together at Mesa Verde. Like most good myths, what actually transpired in the Special World is a bit hard to communicate to those who did not accompany you, a bit vague once you are back in the Real World, and may only whisper at a formal ROI. But the elixir may be the beginnings of a new template for setting scholarly teams with the goals of truly deepening academic experiences and products.

MOVING FORWARD AS A TEAM AND IN HIGHER EDUCATION

And so, the real world. After we all returned to our families, homes, and jobs, we stayed in close contact via e-mail, phone, and in-person meetings. We presented our experiences and findings to several academic associations, both as a team and as individuals within our own professional academic silos. As we all worked on different research projects and publications, our meetings became less frequent for a time, and I remember remarking to my husband that I really missed the Mesa Verde team. There was something that occurred when we were working together (whether freezing in a campground or presenting to a conference at which several attendees became outwardly and profoundly emotional and supportive of our work) that was truly stellar. Don't get me wrong—I have been blessed with some amazing collaborators, friends, and experiences as a documentary director, but the Mesa Verde team had something that I think none of us had quite experienced in our individual fields or even in previous collaborations.

A few months after our Mesa Verde trips, we all came together again to present at the University of North Texas, located in a college town just north of the massive Dallas–Fort Worth metroplex. We presented poetry, showed large-scale photographs, screened a film, and discussed Mesa Verde archaeology and the historical context of Mesa Verde descendants to a diverse and appreciative crowd. After Porter returned to his home in Santa Clara Pueblo, he sent an e-mail to the team. In this communication, he stated:

> Chain-restaurants, big-box stores, and urban sprawl are not unique to any particular place. Each place also has its own versions of used-bookstores, backyard beer gardens, and Cuban bakeries. However, seeing such an overt flexing of corporate power is rare for me. In Santa Clara Pueblo I can ignore many issues with relative ease. I am not used to being in a place where these issues are tenaciously present. I am left pondering what our endgame as human beings is . . . Needless to say, I think this trip to Denton has had a far greater impact for myself than traveling to the Mesa Verde region. My perspective has widened.

To me this very personal observation of concern threw down the gauntlet and challenged the team to further work.

Higher education is in a worldwide state of crisis and flux. Distress is caused by dwindling budgets, skyrocketing tuition, concerns about the actual value and need of a college degree, and the slipping leadership roles of US graduates. The view from the ivory tower harks back to a much earlier time, when universities were the carriers and bastions of threatened knowledge, where texts of antiquity were saved and treasured. Those of us lucky enough to have a key to the tower often see ourselves as the saviors of civilization and, in our part of the globe, of democracy. Lofty, egotistical premises perhaps, but heady stuff nonetheless.

Pressures from government officials, parents and students, corporations, and other interested parties often see things very differently. Our "customers" do not care that we write pithy articles, conduct research, and recognize and pursue necessary changes in science, technology, engineering, math, arts, business, humanities, and other fields. They certainly do not care that a small group of committed scholars had a small amount of funding and went into the field together to attempt new ways of location-based scholarship. They understandably demand accountability, productivity, efficiency, ROI, and a student body prepared for the jobs of the future. Yet my passion and expertise in the classroom are fueled from creative experience outside of it. Facts I teach my students are not final, but are relative to experience and context. It is time to imagine the impacts of a society that could marginalize creativity to a point of no return. I wonder—is curiosity for its own sake under some new threat?

STORYTELLING, OUTSIDE MESA VERDE

My perception of my own work as an artist and teacher has been altered by this Mesa Verde experience, in that I am more dedicated than ever to advocating for the importance of storytelling. I believe that we *all* are storytellers and am no longer chagrined with this basic term or its role in rigorous scholarship. I have confidence that claiming this need is important to the health and success of each of us as researchers, as academicians in higher education, and as people. In my opinion, the most successful scholar-researcher of the future (whether from science, technology, engineering, math, business, dance, painting, or any other academic field) will be transparent in his or her role as a filter for experiences, facts, memory, hypotheses, and theories. I posit that many times, self-reflexivity and an openness to the flip side(s) of one's own perceptions are key to being a holistic, multidimensional scholar and teacher.

The ecosystem of a story, broken down into its most basic form, is a connection between cause and effect. We are constructed to be impacted by stories. We think in narratives all day long. We create quiet, internal stories of the conversation we had this morning, of cooking dinner, of that road trip we took years ago, of our dog getting old. We are neurologically wired to compose our world's narrative out of disparate events and tether them together in a way that makes "sense."

The importance of "story" is recognizably clear to my own students in documentary media and should be patently obvious to anyone paying attention to the deepening importance of social media as a tool for constructing relationships (whether personal, corporate, political, spiritual, whatever). But the key to good storytelling is that a connection is made between the "teller" and the "listener/receiver."

Recently, I was asked to take part in a "distinguished lecture" series at my university, based on my own work. This session was sponsored by the Office of Research and Economic Development, which had previously given me a major university award in recognition of my work. My lecture was attended by faculty from outside my home department and several upper-level academic administrators. It was expected that I would show my own research and creative scholarship, and toward the end I did show excerpts from several documentary films I have directed and produced. However, I opened my talk by inviting the audience to go on a different kind of journey with me. I told them I wanted to talk about storytelling.

I proceeded to tell them, in very visual and vivid terms, about the only film I did *not* finish. In short, this film was to be about Arab Muslim women who are Israeli citizens and actively pursuing both higher education and more visible roles in their communities. My crew and I were early in our filming in the northern Galilee region near Lebanon when the Hezbollah-Israel conflict broke out. After hearing explosions in the distance, and with a large high-definition camera on my right shoulder, I went to get a shot of a helicopter quickly heading toward the northern Israeli border. The helicopter quickly turned, hovered over us, and pointed slightly downward. After zooming in to get a "good shot" from my camera, I realized that there were rocket launchers hanging off the bottom of the military craft and that it certainly must look like I had a shoulder-mounted launcher in my hands. I quietly directed my crew to slowly put their gear down. We put our hands up and slowly walked about twenty feet away, making a point to stay away from a building with several people inside. We sat down on the rocky ground while the hovering helicopter pivoted to follow us. Eventually, as the explosions in the distance got louder, the aircraft flew up about two hundred feet and departed back toward the north. About a week later, after intense artillery fire with rockets coming into northern Israel, and my crew and I hunkering in bomb shelters with the daughter of the local imam, we evacuated out of Tel Aviv. I have not been back since. The film was never completed.

I then told the audience a story about the only film I produced and had broadcast that I did *not* want to make. Early in my academic career, the regional PBS television affiliate asked me to make a film about death, knowing that my own father was struggling with terminal lung cancer. I respectfully declined, and after several follow-up calls during which I more forcefully indicated I was not interested in pursuing such a film, a commissioning check arrived in my mailbox, substantial payment for producing a film on my father and his end-of-life battle. Absolutely mortified at the gall taken by the station's producers, I called my father to tell him and ask for his sage advice.

After a long pause, his answer was, "Honey, I've been waiting for you to ask me if we could make this film together."

And so I made a film, with and about my father, with footage from the beginnings of his diagnosis to right before his death two years later. This was the film I did not want to make, and which I still get requests for. It allowed my father and me to work together to tell part of his life story and to navigate our strong father-daughter relationship in the face of immense sorrow, pain, and, eventually, gratitude.

As I finished telling this story, I noticed that several people in the university audience were in tears, but captivated. These two stories, simply two of thousands sutured into my own life and my role as a documentary artist, had hit a nerve.

I told other shorter and more mundane slices of my history to ease us out of those emotionally intense ones and then invited the audience members to "join me for a symbolic coffee." The idea was that we had just met, and I wanted to get to know them, one on one. To do so, I had a series of questions about them, which they could choose to answer or not. Without asking anyone to speak out loud, I simply put questions up on a screen and let them read, remember, craft stories of their own lives in their minds.

For anyone used to making presentations, this was a risk. Providing a long, respectful pause while administrators from the provost's office, the research office, the university relations and public relations office, several of my own deans and those from other colleges, and faculty from a wide swath of the university took some time to tell themselves their own stories could have gone badly. I could have "lost control" of my audience. I listened for the squeaking chairs and looked out for the glazed-over eyes.

But the exact opposite happened. They absolutely dug in. I could see it from the podium. It was as if the permission to tell stories was the best offering I could have given as an academic scholar. They were riveted and engaged. And while I did eventually speak a bit about my published scholarship and research, the "storytelling" moments were the takeaway for all involved.

Within thirty minutes after returning from my office, I had multiple e-mails and phone calls from people who had been at the session; I was thanked for giving some space for everyone there to think of themselves, their own stories, their myths, memories, challenges, successes. To think of their lives, their research, their scholarship, and their multidimensional returns on investments in different ways. I know that I was inspired to take this speaking risk because of my work with the Mesa Verde team.

In the end, I know we are among the voices advocating for claiming and celebrating higher education beyond the important and basic principles of job credentials, academic reputation, and silo-based productivity. Maybe we can be all of these yet anchor our tendencies in respect and larger universal curiosities. My hope is that the various stakeholders in higher education can move forward more holistically if we occasionally go into the field with no specific ROI other than to listen and experience. Perhaps this particular research team is among those influences offering a new directional sign or two. Perhaps it is time for a reset.

The film is available to view on the *Sushi in Cortez* book page at the University of Utah Press website, www.UofUpress.com.

6

Fire in the Rain
Exploring the Moral Terrains of Mesa Verde

Robert Melchior Figueroa

SPIRAL CAVE

After a very cold night with isolated moments of sleep under wind, rain, and snow, there's nothing like stepping out from my tent and directly facing that cold wind, rain, and snow. And a canyon wall at Mesa Verde National Park Campground. With all the amenities of contemporary campsite life, despite the hard bed and the constant feel of being part of an extended and glorified picnic, it does seem appropriate and even fair to be slapped with a bit of the Colorado Plateau weather to remind us it's not always blue skies, pines, glowing canyons, and billowing clouds. Just so, in the cold snow-rain, we need to get someplace dry enough to think. We decide to make our way down to Cortez for coffee, thawing, and regrouping. Laptops and smartphones active in the coffeehouse, we check the weather and decide to make for Butler Wash, Utah, an easy switch of the itinerary for the next several days and only two hours away to find that place where storms move on.

The clear blue and new white clouds pass along this canyon where the storm has left crisp air. Step back carefully and a spiraling cave outlines the large portal in the top of a natural bridge. Standing under the natural bridge, we look across the small canyon to the cliff dwellings of this site in the Mesa Verde region currently called Butler Wash. The cliff-side drop under the natural bridge is deceptive because of the upward vertical attraction the spiraling cave gives before us; taking any more steps back is ill-advised. The ceiling portal spirals out to the sky, and back again through that portal from the skyscape are traces down along the wall left by the millions of former water flows that stained concentric circles into

118

Rob Figueroa climbs ladder at Balcony House, Mesa Verde.

Handprints at Butler Wash.

an ever-spiraling place where a small pool forms. Taking half-steps back-ward against the naked gravity, I can see hand markings on the wall of the cave. Pivoting to the canyon, I can see the cliff dwelling directly across the canyon and that the messenger would have seen that dwelling while mak-ing the markings.

Porter Swentzell shares with me a true story. The hand markings con-vey a coming and going of people from this place. These markings are actu-ally clear forms of communication that are intentional, meant for a specific audience-folk, and carry a distinctive significance from its messenger regard-ing the environmental relationship of a people who live with this place, but not in stasis. Comings and goings are significant enough to communicate over time. The open hands on the wall can be related to the closed hands with the thumb side up. Holding your hand like this makes a spiral. The hands on the wall relate to the spiraling of the closed hand; a right hand on the wall indicates arrival to this place and the left hand the departure. Dis-cussing these signs, we also learn that approaching a cliff dwelling is done by a kind of spiraling in; sure enough, we can now see the worn footholds spin-ning up the canyon wall to make access, arrival, and departure easier and to make it easier to be seen in either direction. In other places, wall drawings would include spirals, and these too can be understood from the shapes of our closed hands; copies of the spiral of the right hand are arrival signs, and those of the left-hand spiral are departure signs. So begin lessons to be learned from one another in this research, beginning with the multitude of ways that our bodies are communicating with culture and place, between our values and the landscapes. These kinds of spirals inspire the experiences I relate in this chapter.

The collaborative transdisciplinary venture of the Mesa Verde Project includes studying ourselves as moral agents traversing a moral terrain of a region within new and habitual practices. We put ourselves under scrutiny in multiple ways to find pathways of knowing and living through one another. My chapter offers a perspective of the environmental philosopher who looks through the lens of environmental justice, personally, politically, and academically.

Regarding the Mesa Verde Project, I am interested in the ways that we establish moral places for the large frame of justice issues in our engagement with one another and the Mesa Verde region, which I term *moral terrains*. In collaboration, I concern myself with the conundrums we all face because we have our own situated experiences, our own professional ones, and our own disciplines that will ward off other ways of thinking and practicing. Collaborations of the type we have built in this research team are *reconciliations* to this tendency to suspend or even block out other perspectives. Each of us informs the other of a perspective on the region and of experiences that describe the moral terrains we traverse. We contend with the limits of knowledge and the ways in which we tell and don't tell in our own fields. Melinda and Steve Bardolph have material to be edited out or images to enhance. They have a filmic and imagery language to convey. David Taylor uses his writing to effect and draw experiences out of the reader while choosing to edit particular words and phrases that could tell a different story. Steve Wolverton faces the archaeologist's dilemma as he shares his discipline for us to muck around in and learn from. Porter Swentzell's generosity is incompatible because we cannot do this work, not ethically we couldn't and not accurately, if we lack his wisdom and input and presence in our work. And, of course, Porter has cultural limits according to the amount that it is appropriate to share with us in this venture.

My concern for environmental justice at Mesa Verde is influenced by my career-long attempts to disclose many contradictions of access, respect, and knowledge in a world where the tourism industry is a high symbol of consumption. For example, little of the Mesa Verde region isn't impacted by the legacy of what can be called "environmental colonialism." My approach is to unravel points of social issues that maintain both subtle and obvious but maintained forms of injustice, especially regarding the environmental heritage and desires of the Pueblo people, as well as the role that archaeology plays in these moral dilemmas. Indeed, I have a tremendous respect for archaeologists, especially regarding the moral controversies between archaeology and respect for indigenous heritage; this became a personal challenge for me to reconcile as a scholar of environmental justice.

DISCIPLINE AND DISOBEDIENCE

Perhaps chafing to the traditional philosopher (primarily of the Western tradition) are the ways that environmental philosophy welcomes interdisciplinary scholarship. To some, interdisciplinarity plus environmental philosophy yields the critique that the resulting scholarship is neither philosophy nor rigorous research. The irony of this is that mainstream philosophy relies heavily upon its interactions with other disciplines. Philosophy should be *the model* of interdisciplinary thinking. I joined the ranks of philosophy majors because it was the one discipline that allowed me to study all the disciplines. Over time, however, I came to realize that "discipline," the term we use to describe small children who do not reach for every eye-catching box in the food aisle, or the quiet children in church, or the noncrier on the airplane, the child with manners, you name it, is closer to the academic meaning of "discipline" than we may think. Discipline is knowing "what *not* to do." Discipline is knowing limits and abiding by them. Discipline is obedience. Ironically, I and many other philosophers took to our field specifically because we refused to be intellectually disciplined in this fashion.

Interdisciplinary work is therefore my perspective, perhaps because of my personality, perhaps because I lack rigor or obedience, but in either case it is the kind of scholar I am—one of canonical training yet committed with self-discipline to disobedience. Yet I am not unique in this approach, as it is difficult for me to find scholars who avoid interdisciplinary research, though their interest usually includes the condition that they can keep the institutional security of a home department.

To make matters worse (from the perspective of mainstream philosophy), the work of the Mesa Verde research team project is representative of "field philosophy," an approach that includes working "out in the field," engaging with an interdisciplinary perspective, and enhancing public discourse. However, one can be in the field and still oddly not work out of the bounds of traditional academia and not work in either an interdisciplinary or a transdisciplinary fashion.

My role? When we prepped over the summer, coteaching and sharing our research, discussion pointed to my role as the teller of the "anti-story." I remain confused about that designation, as it sounds adversarial, and I tend to disobey the tradition of adversarial philosophical exchange. Maybe what was meant was that I would fill the role of providing a "metastory" from the multiple realities, constructions, and beliefs underlying the various stories that we would come to experience and tell, share and change, build and reflect upon. To me, however, each of us has been engaging in unraveling the metastory context as it relates to ourselves. Visual, filmic, poetic, scientific, philosophical, cultural, historical, experiential metastories are the stuff of this book, but they are rooted in our shared experiences.

From my perspective, it was hard to find what, if anything, I would offer the team that was unique and interesting. As a result, I shifted my thoughts from contributing an academic perspective to reflecting upon the privilege of being a part of the team. Any part of it, to go to the field and be in my method, I had to observe and listen, provide humor to fill silence or carry on, to just be. And that is what I did. Unsurprising to me, given my personal history in the region, I experienced insights, healing, inspiration, and laughter and excitement.

PLACING AND ENVIRONMENTAL IDENTITY

To gather a sense of what role I play on this team, its significance for me, and the influence others have upon me, let me indulge in a few spirals about the Four Corners region. There is a deep sense of contingency behind my investment in this project. I have relied upon the Colorado Plateau for personal salvation several times; this is only the most recent chapter in a series of moments that connect my life.

Between 1987 and 2004, I clocked thousands of miles exploring the Four Corners region of the Colorado Plateau. Always with a companion, I have camped and visited, traversing my "regular" spots of the Canyonlands of Utah and finding new places each time. I have visited Native lands of Pueblo, Navajo, Hopi, Ute, and mestizo Mexican Americans, as well as the small towns and hubs of predominantly white populations. As tourist, local, imported resident, and regular passer through, I have come to rely on this region for solace, spiritual connection, hiking, climbing, biking, exploration, existential reset, comfort, and a sense of meaning. I depended upon these places when I was starting out as an adult, when I was homeless, after a tragic love loss, when I needed direction, when I needed to step away from things, to be literally revitalized upon a near-death fall from a canyon wall, when I needed the deepest night sky, and when life decisions had to be made. There are too many stories, but in all that—even after coming across numerous Ancient Pueblo sites—I had only circumnavigated Mesa Verde National Park. How I finally arrived there with this group can be traced to a 1990 moment at a Lake Powell campsite, under a 120-degree heat wave, after weeks of camping in the region to cleanse myself from the burnout of working as a counselor at a crisis hot line for a psychiatric hospital in New Jersey. Then I decided to commit my life's work to environmental philosophy.

Environmental Philosophy and Environmental Justice

Environmental philosophy broke into the intellectual and academic scene in different waves, culminating in solid landing in the 1970s when it crashed against the craggy shores of conventional Western philosophy. Environmental philosophy is now legitimate in academia; undergraduate curricula include courses in environmental ethics (better termed "environmental philosophy"), making such courses regular offerings to satisfy the bachelor's degree in philosophy. Professors are hired who specialize in environmental philosophy, academic journals flourish with scholarship, international conferences abound, and academic publishers run several environmental philosophy projects, including classroom texts, manuscripts, reference series, and edited volumes. Still, the mainstream of Western philosophy holds firm to the ironic idea that it can determine the rigor of one branch of philosophy from another, and environmental philosophy being a newcomer to the tradition still gets questioned as to whether it is "real philosophy."

Within environmental philosophy, I work from the perspective of environmental justice studies. A short definition of environmental justice is the study of social justice in environmental issues that fundamentally requires some interaction with the people facing environmental struggles. Scholarship must be influenced by the voices engaging the struggles. This is what makes environmental justice a transdisciplinary practice: it must draw its sources from outside of the academy and likewise produce results that reach beyond the academy. It must also be transformative, seeking to ameliorate direct injustices and overhaul the systems that continue to produce unjust results. As a result, I am prone to go all the way down to transforming the very nature of justice itself because I realize that justice and environmentalism have to be reframed to address real struggles.

My lifework is soldered to social justice, and I am unable to distinguish social and environmental justice. My agenda is to show that the best way to discover the nature of justice is by understanding ourselves and our struggles as environmentally embedded. Thus, beyond field philosophy, the Mesa Verde team represents an opportunity for transdisciplinary environmental justice studies in addition to the responsibility of working collaboratively with open-minded and inspiring colleagues.

New World

On the opposite mesa from the spiral cave, I sit above the cliff dwellings, looking over the canyon, and extend my view as far as the mountains on the horizon. Porter is standing only ten or so feet away, paying his respect to the place with a ritual that gives me that feeling of solemn respect deserving silence and a pensive, bowed posture. We continue almost in range of conversation, but silently taking in the place and its meanings. Breaking the silence, I shuffle to sit closer to Porter and carefully ask the question that I don't know how to specify: "So, what does this place mean to you?" And we share the fact that we both were looking to talk, but both respected each other's silence, not wanting to intrude on the experience of each.

Porter takes the time to explain to me the complexity of meanings of these cliff dwellings that visitors describe as ruins. The high points to my memory are several. One, the people who lived here long ago are considered to still be here. They are still here in their relations to the place they lived in for so long, in the structures as they left them, in the canyon and the horizon that spreads 360 degrees and extends above and downward, and in the legacy of the histories they leave. Two, the Pueblo, with the exception of particular members who have some allowance and specific roles with the community, tend for a number of reasons to forgo revisiting these cliff dwellings and the Mesa Verde region.

A primary reason for this cultural tendency to restrain from revisiting the region, and the cliff sites in particular, was again actually recalled to me a few months later from the documentary *The Mystery of Chaco*

Canyon (1999), which I caught during some insomniac moment at two in the morning. Paul Pino, a current Laguna Pueblo council member, confers in the documentary what Porter said on the mesa that day, that the Pueblo cosmology has three worlds. The Mesa Verde civilization was a world, the first one, where people lived embedded in their environment for ages and ultimately digressed from the purposeful moral path. I am mincing Porter's wonderful expressions into my own version of the story here, but I believe I'm capturing the gist. The path that dictated how the Ancient Pueblo should have been living was lost to the extent that the people strayed too far from the true path to recover. Having lost the ability to right themselves with their world, it was time for migration to the second world. This impetus spurred the mysterious migration from Mesa Verde to the Rio Grande region, where the Pueblo people now reside.

Porter's account tells me that the mysterious migration is not really so mysterious to Pueblo people. In the archaeological lessons I have enjoyed from Steve Wolverton during our summer teach-ins with the Mesa Verde team, I struggled to understand how archaeologists draw causal connections concerning this migration. Did the communities get too big, hence the mega cliff structures of obvious grand sophistication in organizational structure? Did they lose their resource capacity because of the great drought that extended much longer than they had previously experienced? Did this lead to food shortage or health decay? Did *these* factors lead to defensive postures against neighboring communities who may have needed to encroach upon the resources of others for their survival? And why migrate so far? For Porter and for the shared accounts from Pino in the documentary, all these things are the broken-down causal theories and complexities that non-Pueblo archaeologists and non-Pueblo peoples are disentangling. In contrast, for the Pueblo, all *these* "facts" (and more) can be articulated through the cosmology of a departure from the first world that had gone astray from the moral vision of the people regarding how they related to their world, their environment, and their relationships to humans and nonhumans.

I learned a longer interpretation of this story from Porter that day. The horizon that can be seen from our shared space on this mesa is all part of our world, and if we went to the distant mountaintop on our horizon we would see a more extended horizon; thus, we would be extending our world to those places where our horizons unfold. We would therefore have to go a great distance in order to get to a place that is finally different from the world we occupy. Hence, the Mesa Verde Pueblo would go as far as the Rio Grande region to encounter the second world, leaving the first world far enough away as to avoid the relations of the lives that went astray. This distance would partly ensure that the previous digressions from the path wouldn't be repeated. This story makes clear why the Pueblo do not want the sites of their ancestors excavated and why they forgo revisiting the region or the dwellings of their ancestors. The idea of returning to a world that was left for a better world in the cosmological trajectory is problematic, to say the least. The first world still lives in that place, and we still have obligations to respect it where it lives.

ENTER AN ENVIRONMENTAL JUSTICE PERSPECTIVE

At Butler Wash, I tried to share my account of environmental identity and environmental heritage with Porter in order to grasp how our perceptions and worldviews can be shared, translated, mutually experienced, and developed into our own collaborated and different meanings.

I have always deeply respected and coveted what I learn from my interactions with Native peoples, and I tend be very careful about what, if anything, I share of their thought, lest I trip the line of an anthropologist and commit a violation of environmental colonialism. I write here like a philosopher in environmental justice studies, trying to share how the thoughts Porter and I shared inform the work I do and the experiences I have. I can assure the reader this is not the way that Porter and I fashioned the conversation, which was deeply respected, comfortable, and formative to my relationship with him.

In my work I often deal with what I call *environmental identity* from an environmental justice perspective. This pertains to the identities of people as they are wedded in their relations with their environment. I argue that all meanings and behaviors people have toward their environment (which is understood in the broadest terms) relate directly to meanings of justice. *Identity* helps to capture that sense of individuals and communities as recognized socially and politically in their environmental relations. People are shaped and made by their environments, and this is reciprocated by how people shape values and behaviors. *Environmental heritage* is this process over time, in which a collective environmental identity is inherited from the past with many nuanced values and practices, sometimes not described explicitly in terms of "environmental." The community (including humans and non-humans) inherits the past, presently assesses the meanings of the past in

Rob Figueroa and Porter Swentzell talk on the rim above Butler Wash.

the many ways their lives reveal environmental relations, and then determines (with conscious beliefs and values or just habitually or both) what
values and lifeways to share forward. The forward aspect of heritage is
actually its kinetic cultural energy, since the past is already inherited and
subject to current deliberation for future legacy.

How we live and how we interpret the past combine for our current
environmental identity, and the ways in which we bring them forward or
change them are the justice of concern here. If a community is unable to
find and voice its environmental identity and its vision for environmental heritage (and these may be multiple identities for one group), such as

eliminating toxic waste, determining land use, protecting sustainable practices, or maintaining inherited environmental knowledge into the future, then recognition justice is being threatened or violated or both. Recognition justice pertains to the conditions and interactions that allow for respect and inclusion of different peoples who are uniquely, differently, and historically situated by their environments and includes social interactions that are usually determined by power relations. To achieve recognition justice, inclusion and shared, equal, and respectful agency between different environmental identities have to be present and realizable.

The narrative of the Pueblo cosmology and its three worlds is a vital environmental heritage that deserves recognition in order for the Pueblo to maintain their own moral agency and self-determination as a collective people. My colleague Kyle Whyte, a Native scholar at Michigan State University, works with environmental justice and Native tribes throughout the United States. His term for describing a critical element of recognition justice and environmental heritage is *collective continuance*. The capacity for collective continuance is a condition for respecting the historical experiences and present values of a people. The Pueblo narrative and their desires to forgo revisiting the former world, as well as having that former world left unexcavated out of respect for the environmental heritage of their ancestors, are a part of the social obligation to recognize the Pueblo's capacity for collective continuance.

An ideal in environmental justice studies is *transformative justice*, which generally means the ability to change the power relations that diminish our capacity to alter environmental injustice into a system of conditions that achieve environmental justice. Thus, transformative environmental justice goes all the way down to rethinking justice itself, which is why environmental identity and environmental heritage have come to play such central roles in my thoughts about environmental philosophy and about the Mesa Verde region.

The Pueblo people's shift from the first world to the second is meaningful for environmental justice because of the impetus to promote a transformative justice. In the case of the Ancient Pueblo, migration to establish a new environmental identity, realignment of the path of civilization, experience of collective agency for continuance, and development of a new environmental heritage is a remarkable achievement in transformative environmental identity. It contributes to features of environmental justice, including recognition, and additionally to reconciliation. The Pueblo explanation of their great migration to the Rio Grande region is an expression of how they transformed their environmental heritage from the first world of the Mesa Verde region to this world in the Rio Grande region. This recognition articulates to the non-Pueblo a traditional environmental knowledge that has reconciled past struggles with present lives.

In the discussion of the Pueblo's migration, non-Pueblo people give a nod to the traditional account as what the Pueblo people believe, but rarely is there sufficient recognition given to the legitimacy of the Pueblo account. In non-Pueblo environmental heritage, there are requirements for causal explanations that are scientifically legitimate: social sciences to determine the organizational reasons people migrated, physical sciences (biology, ecology, meteorology) to invoke the resource reasons people had to migrate, other social and physical sciences to assess what the people were up to prior to their migration as clues to the final results. Meanwhile, the Pueblo express a transformative moral story of environmental relationships and obligations to migrate from a digressing cultural context, and in doing so they still recognize the Mesa Verde Pueblo culture of the past as presently legitimate (that is, still there) in considerations of environmental justice. For instance, the desire to restrain from disturbing or even visiting the cliff dwellings at Butler Wash or Mesa Verde National Park is recognition of the legitimacy of the past peoples who somehow still occupy those spaces in the moral and environmental cosmology.

Indeed, Mesa Verde incurs other transformations for non-Pueblo people. We, non-Pueblo, visit the cliff dwellings, and the current areas of the national park and other public lands participating in a national idea of preservation and an economic idea of tourism. As a result, we may experience transformations in our own environmental identities. The challenge for the environmental justice scholar is deliberating which transformations best achieve justice. Is the deeper meaning of justice better served by my personal transformation at experiencing the cliff dwellings through my touristic gaze? Or is it better served by communicating with others who have different moral perspectives and learning their environmental identities in order to respect their concerns to leave these sites alone? These are not necessarily mutually exclusive, but they are the pivot point from which I must seriously consider aspects of environmental justice that relate to a preferred transformation.

Rob Figueroa walks inside Balcony House.

A PARALLEL ACCOUNT OF MORAL TERRAINS AND ENVIRONMENTAL JUSTICE

During our field research in the Mesa Verde region, a perspective of Porter's was repeated several times in different contexts, and it has been given some attention by members of the team in this collection of essays. Melinda mentioned her pride in this collaborative group when Porter stated our difference from researchers he knows who approach a situation seeking knowledge and from that gain respect, whereas he tells us that the Pueblo approach first with respect and from there gain knowledge. This was also part of our conversation on the mesa at Butler Wash, and he presented this perspective in our public talks at the University of North Texas and in Denver before the Society for Ethnobiology. We all received this perspective with great consideration and reflection. To distinguish knowledge and respect, to distinguish it in cultural approaches, and to see it present itself in our fieldwork raises many tumbling thoughts for someone working in philosophy.

The process of respect to knowledge rather than knowledge to respect has implications for different cultural attitudes toward accumulating knowledge and how we come to treat one another. Consider this in light of my interpretation of some exchanges we experienced during our Mesa Verde fieldwork and its parallel with similar work I have done in Australia.

WE SHARE SO WE CAN UNDERSTAND

In Arnhem Land, Northern Territory, the part of Australia where regional Aboriginal authorities grant permission for outsiders to enter for only a specific amount of time, I toured the ancient rock drawings at Injalak Hill with elders of the Gunbalanya community. One of the elders who guided me and my students fondly repeated, "We share so that we understand; we cannot understand if we do not share." His sentiments expressed that sharing information of his people's heritage is an act of mutual respect, and it includes consideration for that which is not shared, that which in his culture, whether because of rules of his community or the historical experience of colonial abuse following shared information, is something that would cross moral boundaries of respect if we further pursued the issue.

Elsewhere in the Northern Territory, at Uluṟu–Kata Tjuṯa National Park, is the large red monolithic rock that the long-existing (at least forty thousand years) Aṉangu Aboriginal community refers to as Uluṟu (though for decades it was known by its colonial name, Ayer's Rock). The Aṉangu have a moral custom written into their oral tradition and now written on a large sign at the base of Uluṟu: "We Do Not Climb." It signifies for the Aṉangu that only certain members of their community, after certain rites of passage have been achieved, can climb the rock. It has always been this way for them according to their environmental heritage. The rock carries multiple layers and significant cultural functions: as a moral map, an ecological guide, and a conveyor of the Dreamtime stories that teach Tjurkurpa, the law of the Aṉangu. If you walk around the base of the rock with a good tour guide, either an Aṉangu elder who has a younger member of the community to translate into English or an informed and respectful non-Aṉangu guide, you will learn some of the Tjurkurpa— basic stories and moral laws of the community—that are permissible to convey to outsiders. Even these few stories teach the tourist how to read some of the rock. Pockmarked and honeycombed parts of the rock face are quickly transformed into the skull of a man (Mala Man), or the paw prints of the dingo who engaged in some conflict, or the mother snake protecting her eggs. With these animals (the human is one of the animals), stories tell of basic moral lessons that include the behavior of some animals and their relations to this land, obligations between family members, and the Aṉangu history.

A common frustration of commonwealth Australians and tourists since the time they arrived on the continent is that stories are told with specific consideration to the audience, that is, whether the audience is a community member, a member of a particular family, as well as the member's gender, age, and function in the community determine who can know what information. Outsiders therefore get very basic information, since they haven't the appropriate member status. Westerners and other outsiders look upon this "secrecy" with great suspicion. It is difficult to discern what others know or to determine if they know anything that would legitimate their opinion of the matter if they won't divulge what they know. The authority to say "I know something, but I can't tell you" is quite suspicious in Western cultures. Aboriginal peoples are well aware of the suspicion and the colonial expectation that seekers of knowledge are inherently entitled to it. This translates directly to a cultural expectation that we are first entitled to knowledge and then we entitle respect, rather than the other way around, as Porter expressed.

Of course, there is the added dimension of environmental colonialism, pertinent to environmental justice long before the concept was even used or fully developed. Indigenous people have shared quite a bit of traditional knowledge with outsiders over historical periods, only to have that knowledge strategized against them for appropriation of lands, resources, traditional ecological knowledge, and assimilatory purposes. Where knowledge had been ignored for these purposes, it was often deemed uninformative, primitive, and even heretical to Western religion and science. Simultaneously, ignored information, appropriate use of shared knowledge, and moral pleas of respect were trumped by the broader agenda to wipe whole cultures clean off the moral terrains of place and history.

Outside of the Anangu community, all visitors to the park know that the Anangu desire that tourists not climb, and the reason is conveyed as a traditional one. But if I am truly outside of that tradition, then where are my obligations to defer to it? And besides, since the creation of the national park, tourists have been permitted to climb the rock with support chain rails. Subsequently, among many commonwealth Australian citizens, visiting the red center of the nation and climbing Uluru have become a nationalist-styled rite of passage. Even after the land of the park was given back to the Anangu during the late 1990s, which was followed by a joint-management structure between the Anangu and the commonwealth, the climb remains open. The intricate policy of joint management and complexities of touristic, moral, cultural, colonial, and indigenous values surrounding the controversial climb are some things I have tried to study from a field philosophy approach with my colleague Gordon Waitt, a cultural geographer from the University of Wollongong.

In order to make sense of these complexities, Gordon and I developed a language of terms under our rubric of *moral terrains*.[1] In short, the idea is that the landscapes upon which we live are terrains of multiple moral perspectives. For the most part day to day, we may follow the moral terrains without too much conflict and forget the ways that we embody our ethics and values in an affective exchange with permissions, instructions, membership, habit, and deviance. The classroom, with its rows and authority at the head, consists of bureaucratically arranged seats for the students to be educated by an expert. This is a moral terrain that presumes tremendous enculturation, such as who can speak when, with what authority, and what allowances. Places like national parks are riddled with different, crisscrossing moral terrains depending upon the situated knowledge and values of the individual visitor. For instance, compare how the visitor perceives her own project and embodiment at the park, including the objectives of tourism, which are many, with touristic consumption, which is often contradictory to lessons learned from the ecological moral terrains. The situated individual brings with her a myriad of collective identities and lenses through which she engages the park, the landscape, the other people, the rangers, the park authority, the mission of the park, and the range of her personal feelings.

A parallel issue of moral terrains applies to Butler Wash, Mesa Verde National Park, and the Ancient Pueblo lands. Having someone with (an intimate) knowledge to better explain what I am looking at in the rock face at Uluṟu or Injalak Hill, or in the cliff dwellings of the Ancient Pueblo, gives me more than the verbal knowledge; it actually shifts my orientation in terms of all my senses. My projected sense of taste is brought into the affective and visceral values I experience in these moral terrains as learning what people ate on Injalak Hill twenty to fifty thousand years ago by reading ancient rock art or at Mesa Verde a thousand years ago by the analysis of artifacts and residues. In both cases, seeing the potential permanence of markings on rocks with dyes from available plants and rock carvings enhances my sense of sight with the story of the place. Surely, I cannot taste the foods at Gunbalanya (Injalak Hill area) from twenty to fifty thousand years back in exactly that way of the past, although I did enjoy eating kangaroo and barramundi during my six months of life in

Rob Figueroa points to petroglyph at Mesa Verde.

Australia, and I quite like to get barramundi here when it's possible, which reminds me of my travels and lessons. But my point is that in a fashion similar to the ways that I visit another culture and try one of its native cuisines by knowing what people eat, I get a visceral sense added to my knowledge. In this way, tourists in national parks make all sorts of visceral moves as they traverse the moral terrains. To share a term with Gordon Waitt, we may refer to these as examples of our "visceral ethics."

As another example, at Mesa Verde, Steve B., Steve W., and I took the petroglyph trail out from Spruce Tree House cliff dwelling that involved some physical exertion up a large-stepped trail. At the petroglyphs we scaled a rock face to climb onto a ledge where the apparently out-of-reach petroglyphs could have been created, but in attempting to use the physical terrain available we surmised the artist must have made the petroglyph upside down. This exercise required a lot on the part of our embodiment and opened a new visceral plane from which we could grasp the process of the petroglyph drawings.

A path determines the perceptions of touch, sight, sound, smell, and taste; values compound with these perceptions to mark other affections such as joy, pride, wonder, anger, fear, despair, and so on. A student who was part of my Uluru research came to the rock with the excitement to see it, then took a base-walk tour, and after hours of learning the rock from Aboriginal perspectives and geological inspection came upon the foot of the climb, and he reported anger at seeing people climb and despair at being mistaken by the traditional owners as one of those tourists who would climb the rock: this was his transformative experience. From this range of moral terrains, there are moral gateways that open and close depending upon the situated ethics we relate to, and the climb itself can be interpreted as a controversial moral gateway to enter the colonial ethic violating the desires of the Anangu or a gateway to openly demonstrate respect by choosing not to climb even without some law enforcement official standing guard to prevent climbing. Such presence of law enforcement to restrict climbing is maintaining the colonial authority of enforcement that the Anangu had long suffered; thus, they believe *true respect comes from self-initiated restraint* rather than imposed restraint by park officials. In the case of my student, the moral gateway of respect for the Anangu's wishes unearthed anger and a visceral response rooted in his self-initiated (with lessons from the guide) respect.

Mesa Verde National Park shares many of these elements of moral terrains. There are extensive layers of moral gateways to access aspects of the cliff dwellings and the environmental surrounds. The broadest construal of the moral gateways relates to Porter's explanation as to why many Pueblo do not "go back" to these dwellings, going back to the first world where moral gateways should not be reopened. Our research group traversed many of these moral terrains by taking tours that involve differential rather than absolute uniform knowledge about the sites. Melinda shared her experience of different tour guides relating distinctive interpretations of the Pueblo people as either war savvy and aggressive or peaceful depending upon the specific tour guide at the same place. As she

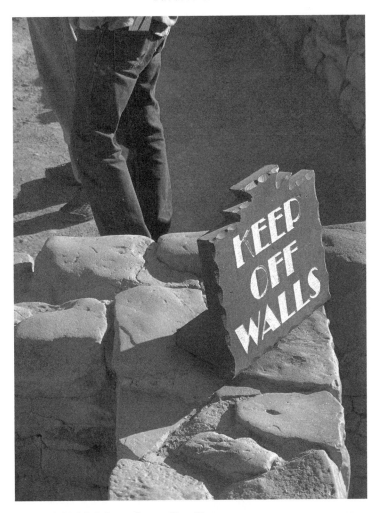

"Keep Off Walls" sign at Spruce Tree House.

observed, different genders of the respective guides only magnified the way that moral terrains, moral gateways, knowledge, and respect unfolded during the tours. The male park official relates a heritage of aggression, whereas the female official conveys the lifeways of a peaceful (nonaggressive) civilization.

At the Spruce Tree House cliff dwelling, there are many shared moral objectives to preserving the site. Staying off the walls, not climbing certain ladders, or not walking into certain areas represents respect for the preservation of these magnificent structures and as much of the ancient culture and living cultures as possible. One sign reads, "Do Not Enter,

Archaeologist at Work." Any inadvertent dust kicking, marks, or what have you would potentially undermine the research going on here. Without the archaeological information, the guides wouldn't get the accurate information to tourists, which we have seen remains differently relayed nonetheless. Without the archaeological information, many things would go on unknown. Yet a different sign may be necessary to address environmental justice as related to the Pueblo people: "Stay Out of the Site! Moral Gateways of Disrespect May Be Opened."

A ranger at the site who enthusiastically shares all he can to onlooking tourists recognizes Porter as a Pueblo person and asks Porter about it, and the moral gateways swing open. For quite a while, Porter is joined by two rangers exploring the place and sharing what they know or can gather about the different rooms and spaces and walls and markings all over Spruce Tree House. As members of Porter's entourage, the five of us are able to access the site past the drooping chains, past the signage: "Keep Off the Walls" and "Keep Out, Archaeologist at Work." After all, one of our members *is* an archaeologist at work, and as associates we can be trusted not to disturb whatever that archaeologist was doing.

As we entered the parts of the structure that were not for public consumption, one of the chains wasn't put back up, and a boy tried to follow us in, only to be prevented by the ranger. Why us average-looking tourists and not him? Because we had privileged access to a moral gateway to knowledge about Spruce Tree House; however, that gateway was closed to others and also caused a different moral gateway, one of restriction, for the boy. Something tells me that the respect that would have been gained from including the boy in our group would have opened (for him and potentially for us) a vastly different moral gateway—of inclusion. The gateway of the boy's interaction with those who see the spaces as significant to living ancestors and with the enthusiasm we all shared for these otherwise "forbidden" moral terrains would have surely produced *great respect*. This is how we could teach respect before knowledge, but the respect the boy learned was the authority of restriction rather than the cultural respect of the place from inclusion.

ARCHAEOLOGISTS, PUEBLO PEOPLE, AND MORAL TERRAINS

A further parallel of moral terrains pertains to the relationship of respect and knowledge at yet another level. At the Crow Canyon Archaeological Research Center, Porter offered his perspective again among the group

Behind the wall at Spruce Tree House.

and our generous colleagues there who stopped working to share conversation. This conversation was particularly important given the fact that there is some contention between the Pueblo (and other tribes) and archaeologists regarding the moral terrain of excavation. "But," said one of our new colleagues, "the more we know from this work, the more respect we can have." There it is, the paradox of this moral terrain we call Mesa Verde archaeology. Note, had I or others of our team raised this issue, it would seem academic and ultimately would be discussed on the abstraction of ethics; however, because we interacted organically as a group, Porter's contention as a Pueblo person raised the moral issue to a genuine human issue much deeper than an abstraction among white researchers.

The living descendants of these excavated places ask that archaeologists refrain from excavation, not unlike the Anangu request, "We Do Not Climb." But an archaeologist can and does defend this activity out of a desire to gain more knowledge and thus to attain greater respect for the descendants. I left the conversation wondering which perspective opens more positive moral gateways and access to particular sites for these archaeologists—the cause of knowledge or the cause of respect?

Do we know more about Pueblo people from excavation? Is the average American, or even the average archaeologist, able to respect Pueblo people more given the knowledge gained from excavations of their heritage? Does information about the Pueblo ancestry by controversial excavation lead to more respect? Which Pueblo are we learning to respect from this invasive activity, the present Pueblo, the Ancient Pueblo, the many Pueblo communities, the Hopi, the Zuni, the Santa Clara Pueblo specifically . . . ? If the Ancient Pueblo, then what moral compass do we use to determine that respect? Certainly, the present Pueblo have made the reading of their moral compass quite clear through their desire for these places not to be disturbed. From an environmental justice perspective, the Pueblo moral compass is being inverted, and the playing field for the decision-making process regarding these sites is not level, since the digs continue with higher regard given to the moral compass pointing to the interests of archaeological knowledge.

The archaeological moral compass entails a different route to respect, and the controversy between these perspectives is better explained by two different paths to two different respect destinations. Whereas archaeologists claim respect for the Pueblo, the archaeologists also consider another target for their respect, science, something the Pueblo do not include (at least not as a priority, and not necessarily in the Western definition of science) in their meaning of respect or in their moral compass. Perhaps the added component for the archaeologist is that through active research, one gains a greater sense of why we so respect our scientific knowledge and methods. This gives us greater respect for our disciplines and *their* own traditions, as well as our academic activities that often receive criticism from nonacademic social arenas. Academics must make a case for their activities in grant proposals, to publishers, to each other, and to the general public with all its own corners of suspicion regarding academic activities and expended resources. In effect, we can ward off suspicions at the first personal level (where we might, say, identify with Porter) if our scholarship gains us more respect as researchers, by our discipline, by our national and international organizations, and ultimately by sectors of the public that find our research informative and intriguing.

However, beyond this specific self-respect for ourselves as researchers and academics, there is a much broader notion of respect at play about the human past. Archaeology, I could also argue, presents those of us outside of the discipline, including the general public, with remarkably important information about the human past. The knowledge unearthed is valuable as a deeper insight into how humans have lived and the distance they have come through the spirals of time and diversity. If this is how we view archaeology, then archaeologists have a vital moral function for humanity indeed. The unearthed past is of great significance for living humans. And if this is the virtue of archaeology, then it is not so far from the Pueblo or any other community that strives for collective continuance by adhering to the respect for their past in their specific cultural heritage.

The moral problem, and I would argue the issue for environmental justice, is that we gain insight into the controversy of respect and knowledge that plagues our current historical condition, which has inherited so many subtleties of colonialism. Working from the broadest human scope of the virtues of archaeology, we are now in conflict between what an individual culture or community wishes according to its value of respect (do not excavate our past peoples) and the totality of humanity (unearth the insights of human civilizations for the benefit of shared humanity). I may be overstating the virtues of archaeology, but for the sake of argument we can see similarities in the respect for the past as a vital moral purpose for present peoples. Thus, the problem is in adjudicating these two moral compasses and deliberating who deserves a greater respect given similar viewpoints that play out in a variety of contexts. Should the practice of sharing humanity's past override a culture's request to not share its past? The view from environmental justice, especially the theory of environmental justice that I advocate, incorporates several elements of consideration to resolve this dilemma.

First, the recognition of the specifically affected parties, especially those whose traditional cultural values and lifeways are affected, has a particular priority that I call the *principle of immediacy*. The priority can be offset if it leads to great harms. Nonetheless, the group most immediately impacted by a decision should have as much direct participation in the decision-making process from the beginning as any other party. If I understand the process correctly, determinations of which sites are of particular interest may often be made by an archaeologist who works through a process that includes getting Pueblo permission or consultation, but note that the Pueblo may be consulted after a series of decisions are already made. This is a problem because questions, conclusions, research trajectories, and agendas are already virtually set (if even potentially in the research vision) before the Pueblo are able to participate. Often, these initial processes limit the range of discussion, decision making, and end goals. This actually influences our meanings of respect and knowledge, the priorities of each, and whether certain meanings of these terms are made secondary or considered at all.

Second, indigenous peoples throughout the world are culturally surviving against a backdrop of centuries of colonialism, much of which occurred in the name of universal human access to the natural commons, and this is a cornerstone of scientific colonialism. Especially in the earlier centuries of "New World" colonialism since 1492, this meant that if something was designated as a natural resource, it could likewise be considered part of the natural commons to which all of humanity deserved access.[2] Thus, it was considered only moral luck that Mayan people had particular access to their natural resources, such as maize and other vegetables, in contrast to entitlements to the right of ownership of these forms of traditional ecological knowledge. From the colonial perspective, knowledge held by indigenous peoples was simply part of the natural world, not something that could be tendered like an invention or patent or property. Colonial powers extracted the natural resources, some of which became staples of European cultures, such as potatoes to Ireland, on the grounds that these were goods for universal consumption. Of course, colonial empires did not share these new appropriations universally outside of profits, power, and trade markets. Very little uncalculated compensation ever went back to the indigenous peoples from where these goods came.

None of these goods could come to the "Old World" of Europe and be of use unless relevant environmental knowledge was appropriated from the cultures of the "New World." Environmental colonialism included the taking of the lands, resources, specimens, and vital cultural capital in the form of traditional ecological knowledge from the "New World." Inside of that process was the appropriation of that knowledge, which was quickly turned into the newest discoveries of the most heralded science of its time—botany. Botany allowed the new knowledge to be experimented with in the great gardens emerging from the "Old World." This new knowledge helped diffuse new vegetables and foods into the new colonies and ultimately to disenfranchise both the appropriated new colonies and the already existing colonies of these empires. This is only a snapshot of one element of the many that environmental colonialism wrought, but its significance is that it evolved from the scientism of the period. As long as something could be designated a natural element, such as the natural resource that indigenous people spent considerable generations developing, knowing, growing, and enculturating, then it was part of the global commons of nature that Enlightenment scientism could appropriate.[3] Respect for scientific knowledge reigned over nature, and naturalizing the values and products of the "New World" was a carte blanche to appropriation, constraints, and elimination of traditional environmental knowledge.

Against that historical backdrop, which is part of the environmental heritage of the world in which we now live, we need to consider the continued, albeit diluted, scientific practices that come into moral conflict with indigenous peoples. Specific differences in the colonial impacts on the exceptional diversity of indigenous peoples might be used to make finer points concerning the historical backdrop. For example, perhaps the Pueblo did not suffer in exactly the same way as eliminated cultures or those who have lost critical elements, such as language, or in the same exact ways as did Mayans or other currently existing indigenous peoples. However, these particulars are largely irrelevant because colonial infrastructure, agencies, and worlds have grown around the Pueblo in the wake of these and many more influences. Thus, we have a national park to serve national interests to preserve the remarkable cultural and environmental riches of Mesa Verde. Further, we have international representation in its designation as a World Heritage Site, which implies that Mesa Verde is for all of the world's population to admire. But these infrastructural and symbolic efforts arise in the aftermath of several hundred years of environmental colonialism, which includes the current justification of public preservation and use of the area under threats of modern industrial expansion and cultural objectification of the cliff dwellings. So how should we now look at the global commons and virtues of archaeological excavation against the respect due to the Pueblo?

Consider science itself in light of these considerations of our global heritage of environmental colonialism. The scientific archaeologist gives great consideration to excavation because excavation is destructive and information can be retrieved only once. However, excavation is also culturally sensitive, a fact that many archaeologists recognize, because of the specific moral terrains of specific indigenous environmental heritage. There's no guarantee archaeologists will not excavate a forbidden knowledge or overgeneralize the knowledge gained from their findings. There is also no way to assess how many self-permitted offenses are going to be generated from the

Pueblo people accommodating requests for permission to excavate. As Porter shared with us, the Pueblo tradition does not include moral codes and practices that account for this kind of invasion. There are no specific protocols for excavations of ancestor places, homes, remains, and objects, other than clear, maintained, and culturally deep codes that are typical of the majority of the world's cultures that recognize the sensitivity of digging sacred remains of ancestors. Nor is there a moral calculus to determine which sites would be better (more or less respectful) to excavate. No moral calculus exists for rendering any particular site completely moral to excavate, for how do we develop a metric to stipulate something is more or less forbidden when respect for ancestors is involved? Without the heritage of such moral allowances and traditional knowledge, the default position is as rational as any: "Just don't do it." Otherwise, we require from our own colonial perspective that indigenous peoples rewrite a new metric against their own heritage to accommodate our interests. This moral dilemma that the Pueblo people and many other indigenous peoples face is yet another impact of environmental colonialism.

Alternately, often without a tradition of moral calculus from the Pueblo peoples and without a proportionally vital moral calculus within science (note that science is barely requiring such a rewrite of its own ethical codes), archaeologists must tread the pitfalls and challenges of science's own moral terrains that entail embracing the responsibility of a professional moral dilemma: wrestle with colonial-style insults when gaining knowledge from excavations, no matter how much researchers intend to be noninvasive and how minimal they may be. In other words, without explicit moral guidance in all the complexities, the scientist decides to proceed and make up the rules and respect in the aftermath. In contrast, the Pueblo consider the lack of moral guidance in their traditional knowledge as cause to avoid such actions. In contemporary science parlance, this is referred to as some version of a "precautionary principle"—if research cannot fully estimate the harms involved in the action, then it should not commit the action. In a compatible lack of moral knowledge and lack of enforcement that we found at Uluru, scientism proceeds for the sake of knowledge, while Pueblo and many other local communities that have faced similar confrontations proceed to respect "inaction" (from the perspective of science) for the sake of what they do know and prioritize, their heritage of respect.

During our conversation with Crow Canyon colleagues, Steve Wolverton draws a wedge in the knowledge-respect dilemma by suggesting that science would be wise to consider also what it should not know. Straddling the respect angle, he suggests it could be better to know when questions shouldn't be asked. And this insight brought back to me the dangers of unchecked scientism. If we just chip and chip for knowledge accumulation, then clearly we are going to produce a moral mess where respect is too often habitually suspended in the ironic name of gaining information to provide more respect. This problem is also self-reflexive to our research team. We have all admitted in some way our participation in this major moral dilemma between respect and specific types of knowledge that resonate with colonial presumptiveness. We ourselves are indulging our research in this accessible region of a long-existing environmental heritage. The park, Bureau of Land Management sites like Butler Wash, tourism opportunities and facilities, and the gem of Crow Canyon are all there for us to explore, and indeed exploit.

My point in this broad discussion of this moral dilemma *is not to argue for the ceasing of science, much less archaeology*. Instead, I raise this conversation as a point of the moral terrains we must negotiate, especially in research, but also in our travels, touristic activities, and even daily lives when we are safely back home. Respect in this discussion has been explored in several dimensions to indicate that even respect is a moral landscape of tricky surfaces and footing. Sometimes this kind of respect is considered inefficient because such extended conversation takes too long. Sometimes it is stifling and can be resolved only in the style that Steve W. pointed out, that is, by not asking. Or take the Aboriginal elder, for whom sharing is an obligation for mutual understanding against any entitlement to expect an indigenous culture to share everything. Or, as Porter suggests, don't excavate. Respect always requires a deeper reconciliation of conflicts than traditional Western philosophy could fully explore because lived dilemmas are the fullest experiences for learning respect. My pitch in this exploration of moral terrains between knowledge and respect has been to show the signposts that emerge from environmental justice with the inspiration that reconciliation between competing values fosters human flourishing in ways in which we have not fully indulged ourselves. In this case, what is to be gained is deeper recognition of environmental heritage and identities over the value of certain types of knowledge at certain times and under certain conditions and procedures.

David Taylor, Melinda Levin, and Steve Wolverton shivering at Mesa Verde campground.

FIRE IN THE RAIN

On our first day of the trip as a whole team, we find our campsites at Mesa Verde National Park in near-dark conditions with a mix of wet snow and very cold rain. We set up our tents and layer up for the night of unforgiving weather. Not two days ago it was in the seventies here and perfect weather, but that is now a distant past to these conditions. I've only just met Steve B. and Porter in person; there's an experience of fresh friendship and common challenge. After the setup, the team huddles for an attempt to get the fire going and get to know each other better. We began our journey to respect over the summer of Skype meetings and exchanges of our respective lessons, but that was only one piece of the puzzle for what we are doing and how we will work together. Building a warming fire in the snow and cold hard rain isn't exactly the way we imagined fieldwork. In fact, my camping experiences in the Colorado Plateau for more than twenty years remind me that this is an impossible task: fire in the cold rain. As we all huddle together at friendly ease despite the conditions and the cold darkness coming fast into the canyon, Porter astounds me with a small fire that is alive and well. A bit of sharing about his family in their role as winter people demonstrates his specific obligation to provide warmth to the people around him. We are now warming—not drying, but warming—but only on the sides of us that face the small, anxious, tenacious fire. Then we randomly and individually turn ourselves around to get the other half of our damp, cold bodies warm.

There are so many metaphors to absorb from our experiences that took place over the next few days, but this one best captures the kind of research we are doing: fire in the rain. We are absolutely enthusiastic, invigorated by one another, collectively fired up against a world and tone of academia that would more likely rain upon our energies than support them. Our methods can be labeled, but we avoid that to respect the spirit that enflames our research. Our goals and return on investment are burning for evidence of productivity, but that should be doused by all means, as long as possible, so that some discovery doesn't get hampered in the prematurely laid details of "results." However, this is an astounding fire that doesn't quit even in the cold, slapping rain, because the small pieces of wood collaborate enough intensity to keep the light alive. For me, this is our little fire, living to learn and challenge the depths of environmental colonialism we face and wrestle within our particular environmental identities. And though we are singular pieces of wood pulled from our own little comfort zones, we have been gathered by forces to battle the given environmental conditions, those we've inherited from our time in history. We are here to build productively in our own right, despite past experiences, and to impact others around us with the flame of inspiration, even if they can be warmed only by the prospects and insights with only half of their person at a time.

NOTES

1. G. Waitt, R. Figueroa, and L. McGee, "Fissures in the Rock: Rethinking Pride and Shame in the Moral Terrains of Uluru," *Transactions of the Institute of British Geographers*, n.s., 32, no. 2 (2007): 248–63; R. M. Figueroa and G. Waitt, "Cracks in the Mirror: (Un)covering the Moral Terrains of Environmental Justice at Uluru–Kata Tjuta National Park," *Ethics, Place, and Environment* 11 (2008): 327–48; R. M. Figueroa and G. Waitt, "Climb: Restorative Justice, Environmental Heritage, and the Moral Terrains of Uluru–Kata Tjuta National Park," in "Ecotourism and Environmental Justice," special issue, *Environmental Philosophy* 7, no. 2 (2010): 135–63.

2. D. L. Kleinman, *Science and Technology in Society: From Biotechnology to the Internet* (Malden, MA: Blackwell, 2005).

3. Ibid.

Epilogue

Whither (wither) interdisciplinarity? At this point, we could provide you with a carefully crafted definition of interdisciplinarity, one that would satisfy those in the academy who require such things. We could state the promise of interdisciplinary research, but we are not interested in *those* answers to the question above, given our experiences together. Rather, we are keen to offer some observations related to our shared experiences. We entered this project wielding interdisciplinarity as a powerful, contemporary approach to doing scholarship; we are not certain that we leave the same way. Looking back, we ask, "Who does interdisciplinary research?" We have agreed in our recent discussions that monikers such as "interdisciplinary poet," "interdisciplinary artist," and the like are somewhat ludicrous. No poet, filmmaker, or painter would claim to be interdisciplinary. They would claim to be creative, curious, and perhaps even free. Yet how does an archaeologist or an ecologist go about pursuing interdisciplinary research?

Steve Wolverton's research that focuses on molecular food residues from fragments of archaeological cooking pottery requires a team that includes analytical chemists, molecular biologists, and archaeologists. Is this research interdisciplinary? It depends on the scale; certainly, this research spans different disciplines of science, but the goal has always been to answer archaeological research questions. Members of the team certainly consider this research to be an interdisciplinary approach to archaeology. It is even easier to recognize David Taylor's and Melinda Levin's various projects as interdisciplinary. In David's work, literature is fused into ecological scholarship; particular examples include the many projects focusing on Texas rivers. In similar fashion, Melinda's films

Back porch at Edge of the Cedars.

about rivers, ranches, even death require engaging multiple disciplines. David and Melinda embrace and claim that their work is interdisciplinary. Would calling them interdisciplinary poems and films make them more valuable? Does the fact that Rob Figueroa's research on Uluṟu is cross-cultural and includes perspectives of a geographer and philosopher increase the merit of what needs to be said? Certainly, the ecologists working with David recognize the work as interdisciplinary because of the novelty of including a nature writer/poet on a team of scientists. Perhaps poetry, films, prose, and artistic photos are simply creative and curious. Perhaps for David, Melinda, and Steve Bardolph, "interdisciplinarity" is simply business as usual.

The point here is that scientists seem to more readily claim the moniker "interdisciplinary." For the archaeologist, the ecologist, or chemist, it is a big deal to cross these boundaries. In discussion of this tendency, we notice what many others have studied in great detail, that scientific disciplines have become increasingly compartmentalized. Undoubtedly, the goal of science to control inquiry through experimentation and precise argumentation has promoted this particularism. The more finely the pie of science is divided, the more control one perceives that can be gained. However, such control is partially illusory, developing as the scholar becomes progressively more embedded in a singular thread of learning. That illusion of control has the negative effect, in our opinion, of a loss of perspective. It may also constrain research to such a degree that curiosity and creativity are greatly reduced. So we speculate that scientists yearning for broader perspectives are likely to recognize and wear the cloak of interdisciplinary research because it pulls their narrow thread back into the warp and weft of humanity.

There is a problem with this cloak, however. Scientism, or the propensity to view science as *the way* to do scholarship, holds powerful sway in American society. Here we are speaking mainly about the *process* of inquiry, but we acknowledge that many of the contemporary tools of the artist and even the poet incorporate advanced technologies produced from science. Our point in terms of the process of inquiry, however, is that to add the moniker *interdisciplinary* to science is to extend the tent of science into humanities, arts, and even other human cultures, thus making them part of science. Meanwhile, returns on investment are recognized mainly in terms of science. The poet, photographer, artist, indigenous person, and others were simply going about their business, doing what they do. Their work has always been creative, free, curious, and at least to some degree interdisciplinary. Now these are valued because they have been colonized by science. The philosopher nods his head, "Yes, this is what has been happening." The archaeologist is humbled and embarrassed, and the Native person may think, "Again?!" "Notsofast!" chimes in the poet; "artists in universities bear some responsibility too." They often seek academic legitimacy and funding by opting for ROIs under the umbrella of interdisciplinarity, broader impacts, outreach, not to mention affiliation with science. Scholars in the arts and the humanities may seek the security of affiliation with science through becoming interdisciplinary, and scientists may seek breadth, curiosity, and creativity through becoming interdisciplinary. Of course, we are generalizing here, but our experiences together make us mildly suspicious about motivations behind monikers.

What was difficult about the process of interdisciplinary fieldwork does not concern crossing into and out of our home disciplines. Rather, it concerns what disciplines have come to mean in the context of contemporary scholarship. What has been challenging is not where we went together, but what we each know we were to go home to—an increasingly quantified and scientized academia. Scientific reductionism has bled over into academia; while the academy espouses and claims to support interdisciplinary or even transdisciplinary research, it seems to still place parameters around what can fit into these arenas. There we must account for the productivity of our creative process prior to being creative. This constraint has left even the scientist compromised, such that now scholarly success is recognized in the currency of dollars instead of richness of ideas. More often than not, if humanities and arts intersect with scientific research, the former are beholden to the latter. Further, in the scientific community, these combined, more holistic surveys of the entire ecosystem of a process/place/event are oftentimes considered "nonscientific," therefore "nonempirical" and "not as valid." Perhaps it is the prompt from this team that valid analysis of complex structures requires a redefining of both process and end goals. We know that in the United States, the spirit of academia is threatened. We see it at universities, but an infection of cloudiness and distrust has permeated our entire educational system. How long before the foundation crumbles?

We come out of this project recognizing the human gift that shared scholarship provides. We suggest that human curiosity and creativity are better preserved in the humanities and arts. Since our fieldwork, we have witnessed increased investment in science at the cost of opportunities for humanities, arts, and even interdisciplinarity. For example, one of our universities recently terminated its small grant programs, which often funded pilot projects outside of science, for the expressed purpose of funding equipment needs. In addition, the Center for the Study of Interdisciplinarity, which funded this project and incidentally had considerable success garnering federal monetary support, recently had its university support stripped away. Like the novice student, we recognize that it is not our innate ability or intelligence that is sparing; rather, what is lacking is awareness, something that has grown for each of us during this project, something (right or wrong) we hope to have shared in this book.

We tell you these insights not after having read literary, philosophical, and scientific treatises on how to be interdisciplinary or about the benefits of interdisciplinary scholarship. We tell you them after going into the field together. What was a vague sense of unease that creativity and curiosity are being stamped out in the name of ROI is now a focused perspective that even the mantles we claim are not what they seem. We did not become "more interdisciplinary" during our fieldwork; we recognized and claimed our humanity. As we experienced a rich tapestry of curiosity and shared stories, the divisions of our fields began to disintegrate. That left us on firm ground together where one person's limits became someone else's strengths. Our qualifications, particular approaches, and disciplines became vague, and we were left with a newly remembered common ground, our shared humanity, which turns out to be a great place for enrichment of creativity.

Acknowledgments

University of North Texas:
    Center for the Study of Interdisciplinarity
    Department of English
    Department of Geography
    Department of Philosophy and Religious Studies
    Department of Radio, Television, and Film
    Institute of Applied Sciences

Northern New Mexico College:
    Department of History

University of Minnesota–Duluth:
    Department of Art & Design

Crow Canyon Archaeological Center

Society of Ethnobiology

Contributors

Steve Bardolph
Associate Professor
Art and Design
University of Minnesota–Duluth

Robert Melchior Figueroa
Associate Professor
School of History, Philosophy, and Religion
Oregon State University

Melinda Levin
Professor
Department of Media Arts
University of North Texas

Porter Swentzell
Assistant Professor
Institute of American Indian Arts

David Taylor
Visiting Professor of Sustainability
Sustainability Studies Program
Stony Brook University

Steve Wolverton
Associate Professor
Department of Geography
University of North Texas